THE MIRACLES AND RICHES OF GOD

*Autobiography of John Nimley Wulu,
Sr. of Monrovia, Liberia, West Africa
(Founder and Builder of Schools)*

John Nimley Wulu, Sr., AA,BA

authorHOUSE

AuthorHouse™
1663 Liberty Drive, Suite 200
Bloomington, IN 47403
www.authorhouse.com
Phone: 1-800-839-8640

©2009 John Nimley Wulu, Sr., AA,BA. All rights reserved.

No part of this book may be reproduced, stored in a retrieval system, or transmitted by any means without the written permission of the author.

First published by AuthorHouse   1/7/2009

ISBN: 978-1-4389-1800-6 (sc)
ISBN: 978-1-4389-1799-3 (hc)

Printed in the United States of America
Bloomington, Indiana

This book is printed on acid-free paper.

DEDICATION

To the following missionaries: Rev. and Mrs. Jensen; Miss LePeirce, my first alphabet teacher; Rev. and Mrs. John Hurston; Miss Mary Martin and Anna Staford, who took the Good News of Jesus Christ, the gospel message that translated us from darkness to light, to Liberia, West Africa.

To all the Christian brothers and sisters who are preaching the Gospel of Jesus Christ all over the world.

To my dear parents, Waylee Kar-da and Kaye-yor Nei, who brought me into this world. May their souls rest in perfect peace and may light perpetual shine upon them.

To my dear and lovely wife, Mrs. Minnie Wulu, my great assistant who stands by me and through whom the Lord gave us our many blessings and riches, our children.

To our precious children: Elizabeth, Ruth, Emmanuel, John Jr., Francois-Caesar, Solomon, Kaller-Minnie, Demonique-Alexander, Johnnette, and Aaron; our riches from God.

ACKNOWLEDGMENT

My special thanks to AuthorHouse Publications, their editors and support team; to my family for their love and support, and to my daughter Elizabeth who spent many hours helping me type the manuscript to send to the publisher.

I GIVE ALMIGHTY GOD THE GLORY AND PRAISE

THE AUTOBIOGRAPHY OF JOHN N. WULU SR.

A FULFILLMENT OF MY PRAYERFUL DESIRE

CHAPTER 1
EARLY DAYS IN MY HOMETOWN

During the past few years, I have been praying to the Lord to give me the strength to put my life story in writing.

Each time I lay in my bed, the Lord would remind me to get started on my autobiography. And I would share my desire to write with my wife. I am thankful to God for giving me sight that I am able to put my life story in writing. I believe that it is very important that I leave a written record of my life for my children and grandchildren so they can have an understanding of where I came from and how I got this far.

It is my fervent belief that my grandchildren and their children will be very happy to read about their grandfather's life story. So, as I begin to write my life story, I pray to God, the Creator of the universe and mankind that he will grant me the strength I need to write according to His will. As I am about to take on this great task of writing my life story, I pray for God's wisdom, guidance, and understanding.

I have learned to put God first in all I do. I am very grateful to God the eternal One, the father of our Lord and Savior Jesus Christ. Let His name be praised and glorified from generation to generation. May His praise be continually in my mouth for creating and bringing me into this world through my dear parents.

I also give Almighty God praise and thanks for loving us so much that he gave His only, beloved son Jesus Christ, who shared his blood on the cross for the sins of the world. John 3:16 says: "For God so loved the world that He gave His only begotten Son, that whosoever believeth in him should not perish, but have everlasting life."

I am so fortunate to have had parents who loved and cared about me so much that they taught me right from wrong. They taught me to love and respect people in general. They taught me to work for what I wanted and not to take what did not belong to me. I am very grateful for the good and sound advice my parents gave me that made me who I am today.

My parents were Karr-dar Waylee and Kayor Nei. My given name is Wulu.

My parents lived in the hinterland in Liberia. They were aboriginal Liberians. So I am a native Liberian. I am very grateful to the Lord for allowing me the opportunity of knowing my roots.

Liberia is situated on the West Coast of Africa between Sierra Leone, Ivory Coast (now called Cote d'Ivoire), and the Republic of Guinea. The population of Liberia is 3.5 million. Liberia got her independence on July 26, 1847.

Because my parents could not read or write, they could not keep my correct birth date, but what they did to give me some idea of when I was born was to record the season in which I was born and count the number of farm years since my birth. This was how my age was calculated. According to my parents, I was born in the brushing season (farm preparation period for planting), which is the later part of November. Counting the number of farms made after my birth, and the season in which I was born, my birth date is set to be around November 28, 1935.

I am very grateful to God that I know my roots or origins. I got my roots in Liberia, West Africa. I am very happy that my children and their offspring will know their roots. We are originals of Africa.

I thank God for allowing me the opportunity to see both my grandmother De-quiee and my great-grandmother Kor-yor. I lived with my grandmother when I was between the ages of six and seven. She lived in Yonn-Wo Town in the Konobo Chiefdom in Liberia. My grandmother was very kind to me. She knew nothing about school. There were no schools in that town; therefore, I did not attend school. When my grandmother De-quiee passed away, my great-grandmother took me to live with her in Tarley Town, where she had her own little house. After living with my great grandmother for a few months, my mother Karr-dar Waylee came and got me and took me to Say-you-o town, where she had her house.

Say-you-o is a small town in Towarbo Chiefdom in the Tchien District, Grand Gedeh County. This was a small town with less than sixty houses. The town had bush green forest with banana and palm plants all around it. The town had no running water system. We drew our water from the creek. The town had no streets or roads; therefore, there were no cars. There were no electricity, streetlights, or electric or gas stoves in the town—our parents cooked on a wood fire.

My brother David and I lived with our mother. We had two half brothers that lived with their mother nearby. We had a very good mother. She prepared meals for us each day, making sure that we were well fed. Our chief food was rice. We were very young boys. Our mother would go in the bushes with her ax or cutlass, cut wood, tie them in a bundle, carry them on her head to her house, and use them for cooking. For our dinner, she would prepare rice and make palm butter sauce with meat or fish, or soup with a variety of meats. Some days, she would cook cassava roots, yams, or plantains to have with fish and meat in eggplant sauce for dinner. Other foods we ate were potatoes with chicken cooked in okra or beat cassava leaves sauce. We ate beans, palm cabbage, banana, peanuts and much more.

I enjoyed fishing; I had lots of fun fishing with my brothers David, Piere Nimley (Nei) Taley, and other friends in many different creeks near our town. We did more swimming in March because it was very hot. Temperatures were anywhere between 90 and 100 degrees in the area. Liberia has two seasons: the dry season and the rainy season.

I would travel with my friends in the forest and go under the walnut trees to pick up walnuts that fell from them. We would fill our bags with walnuts to take home. Mother had a dryer that she built over the fire hearth in the kitchen. She would spread the walnuts over the dryer to dry. When the walnuts were dried, she would take them down and share them with us children to eat. My mother was very kind to us. She showed her love to us in many ways. She always told us to be honest, respectful, and obedient.

In the dry season (summertime) my parents would brush bush (clear areas in the forest) and make farms in Say-you-o town. I would often help my parents with the farmwork. I believe I was between the ages of eleven or twelve. I would usually use an ax to clear small trees while my mother and father used sharp cutlasses and axes to clear bushes under large trees, sometimes cutting them down. Most of our people in Liberia did primitive farming. We did not have farming equipment or machines to clear thick bush for farming. Everything was done manually using axes and cutlasses.

In Say-you-o Town, our people started brushing or clearing the bushes for farming between the later part of November and March. By March the bushes were dried and ready to be burned. The people would then set fire to them to clear the farm for planting. After the dried bushes were burned up, the women began planting rice, corn, and other seeds on the farm.

I helped my mother during planting time. While my mother was planting the rice seeds, I would apply fire to bushes that were not thoroughly burned to clear them off the area for my mother to plant. After the rice and corn plants had grown to about a foot, it was time to begin planting the cassava plants. My job was to gather the cassava sticks, cut them to about six inches each, and take them to my mother

The Miracles and Riches of God

for planting. While she was planting the cassava sticks, I would begin planting the young plantains.

Another responsibility I had on the farm was to keep plant-eating animals away from the growing plants. On the farm we had problem with animals such as bush hogs, gray monkeys, bush cows, and other animals trying to eat the plants. I had to climb up on a tree stump on the farm and keep watch for such animals. When I saw them approaching, I would yell out for one of my parents to come and drive them away. At night it was my parents' responsibility to watch for the animals using man-made bamboo straw torchlights and cutlasses. The rice and corn were usually ready for harvest by July. July and August are new rice and corn months.

In those days I had no concept of what school was. When I lived in the Towarbo Chiefdom, there were no school buildings in the entire chiefdom. There were six towns in the Towarbo Chiefdom: Say-you-o, Young-bar, Boo-way, You-way, Darwah, and Sire-well Town.

I have traveled to every town in the Towarbo Chiefdom, as well as to other nearby and faraway chiefdoms. Every town was surrounded by green forest. Most of the towns had a great deal of palm trees and banana trees around them. During those days we did not have shoes to wear, so I traveled barefoot with my parents and others from the town. As I mentioned earlier, there were no streets or cars around. So we traveled by foot on paths through thick forests. Other chiefdoms I had an opportunity to see as a young child were Konobo, Par-lebo, Gleeo, and Glar-lo Chiefdoms.

While traveling, we would come across live animals such as leopards, elephants, hippopotamuses, bush cows, deer, and lots of monkeys jumping from tree to tree.

There was one river in the Towarbo Chiefdom, the Dobeh River. A very large river separated our chiefdom from other chiefdoms and towns. There was no bridge to go across the river. To get to the other side of the river, people had to travel in canoes. As a child, I had the

5

John Nimley Wulu, Sr., AA,BA

opportunity of swimming across the Dobeh River, which runs through Konobo Chiefdom too.

I can record that Konobo Chiefdom has two clans: the Bilabo Clan and Barlue Clan. Some of the towns of the Bilibo Clan are Ziah Town, Greegro Town, Dewah Town, Wlorbut, Barrgro, Karwo Town, Zarr Town, Glay Town, and Boulue Town. The Barlue Clan has Bowu Town, Tarley Town, and Say-you-o Town, among others. The Cavalla River separated Konobo and Glio Chiefdoms from Ivory Coast.

In Say-you-o Town, my brother David and I were living with our mother very happily. Our mother, Kar-dar, was very young and was having children. I remember that once my mother was pregnant and gave birth to twins, which did not survive. Shortly after the delivery, my mother got sick. We had no hospitals in the entire chiefdom. And there were no medical doctors, nurses, or any type of medical provisions. Our cousin Yur-wen took my mother to her farm to treat her with native herbs. I was always with my mother wherever our relatives took her for treatment. I loved my mother dearly. It was very hard for me to go far from her side. Although my mother was ill, she continued to advise me to be a good child and never to take anything that did not belong to me, but to always ask for things I wanted.

On Cousin Yur-wen's farm, my mother got no better; the problem got worse and worse. She could not eat any food. I was greatly concerned about my mother's condition.

She was taken back to our town. I began to shed tears. When we got in the house, my mother could not talk and could not open her mouth. The relatives around her began to cry and I started crying too. My mother passed away that same evening. I had never dreamed that my mother would leave my brother David and I in this world all alone. It was a very, very bad and sad day for us. We had seen what we never dreamed would happen to us.

My brother David and I were very young. So it was very painful and sorrowful on our hearts. While crying, I thought to myself, Now that

6

The Miracles and Riches of God

our mother is gone, who will care for us and who will take our mother's place? It took years for me to get over the grief and painful sorrow of my mother's death. When my mother died, my uncles Taley, Waylee Kon, and other relatives came to her funeral, after which my uncle Tarway Taley took me to Konobo Chiefdom to spend some time with him.

After spending time with Uncle Taley in Konobo, it was time for him to go to work at the Firestone Plantation in Maryland County, Liberia. He took me with him. He worked a few months on the rubber plantation and decided to leave. He took me to Uncle Charlie Waylee, who worked for the same Firestone rubber plantation but at Division #5 in Burlobo, near the Cavalla River. My uncle Charlie taught me how to tap rubber trees to get white latex out of the bark.

After learning how to tap rubber, I left and went to live with my cousin at the Firestone rubber plantation, Division #4, in Zinc Camp. I was never interested in tapping work. But my cousin asked me to work as a tapper for about two to three months before going back to Say-you-o Town. He said this would help me earn money to buy a few pieces of clothing for myself and other relatives in the town. So I agreed and worked as a tapping boy on the Firestone rubber plantation in Maryland County, Liberia, West Africa.

When I was on the plantation, I still knew nothing about education. I had no dream of any such thing as school. My thinking was mainly about earning money to buy clothes. If my memory serves me correctly, I earned about twenty or thirty cents a day, which was approximately $6 a month. The Firestone Company gave me one bushel of rice, smoked fish, and pork meat a week. At the end of the month, the company deducted $2 from my pay to cover the cost of food items given to me during the month. This left me with $4 a month to take home. As I mentioned earlier, I was never content with tapping rubber trees. When I found some people who were going back to Say-you-o, in the Towarbo Chiefdom, I left the job and went along. What I did not realize was that hard labor without pay awaited me in my hometown.

Within two months after my arrival in Say-you-o Town, the townspeople asked me to do porter or labor work on the compound of the District Commissioner without pay or food. Not having a mother to speak on my behalf, I agreed and went with the others to work as a laborer in the compound. I would walk miles, carrying thirty pints of rice in a container for me just to have one pint of rice per day to eat.

After two weeks of service on the compound, the Commissioner authorized that the porters, including myself, must go to Sinoe County, a six days' journey by foot to bring back benzene (petroleum) for the use of the radio station located in Zwedru, in the Tchien District in Eastern Province, now called Grand Gedeh County.

I was never pleased with such working arrangements, never pleased to work as a porter, let alone not get pay. As I record, this was my second time serving as a laborer. When I was very young, I was sent to be a waterboy for the big people, or older people, who were opening up the forest and building a transportation road from Zwedru, the capital city of Grand Gedeh County, to Sinoe County.

We began our six days' foot journey to Sinoe County. When we got there, we were taken to a certain area to get the benzene. I and a laborer friend name Wulu were given a small steel can that held six to seven gallons of petroleum to take back to Zwedru. On our way back, I began to seriously think about my life condition. I thought about what to do after my laborer assignment with the Commissioner was completed. I thought about getting a job at the gold or diamond camp, but I had no experience in such areas, so I discarded that idea. Then I thought about going back to work at the Firestone rubber plantation. But I knew I despised tapping work.

My first six children God blessed me with: back - Elizabeth, from left to right Ruth, Francois, John Jr., Solomon, Emmanuel, my wife Minnie, and myself

Me as a young man

Papa Wulu college graduation class, 2nd person from the right

Two additional children added to the family. Back - Elizabeth, left to right - Ruth, John, Papa & Mommy Wulu, Francois, Emmanuel. Front left to right: Kaller, Solomon, Johnnette

Left to right Solomon, Johnnette, Caesar-Francois, Mommy and myself

My graduation picture from the University of Liberia

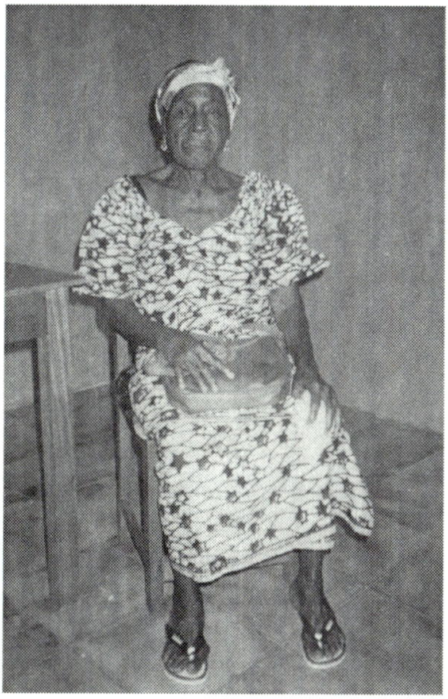

My sister-in-law, Noon Kalor

Papa Wulu

Papa and Mommy Wulu

Papa Wulu

ABOVE: Papa Wulu and daughter Elizabeth

LEFT:My Father's Day picture in July of 1986. I was honored Father of the Year in Monrovia, Liberia

My wife and I are standing in front of our car

Our ten children the Lord blessed us with. Back - Elizabeth, Aaron. Left to right: John, Ruth, Mommy & Papa Wulu, Francois-Caesar, Emmanuel. Front Left to right: Solomon, Johnnette, Kaller, Demonique-Alexander

John Wulu, third person from the left.

Chapter 2
God's love,
He Answers Prayers

Once as a child, I saw white missionaries come to my town. I saw them kneel down, bow their heads, and pray so God could help us. On our way to Zwedru, we stopped in a town to sleep, and I thought of what I saw the missionaries doing in my town.

When everyone was asleep, I went in a corner in the house, knelt down, and began to do what I'd seen the missionaries doing. I began talking to God. I said, "God, please show me where to go, show me the way. I do not know which way to go, direct me, God I pray." I did that secretly because I did not want anyone to know what I was doing.

We got to Zwedru and delivered our small steel can of benzene to the radio station. We were told our job was completed and that we could go back to our various towns. We were pleased to end the assignment. We went to the Commissioner's messenger's house to rest for a couple of days before heading to our various towns. After resting for a couple of days, the other boys were getting ready to go. I, on the other hand, was not thinking about going back; instead, I was thinking about what I could do so I wouldn't have to be a porter or laborer for the rest of my life and wouldn't have to work for the District Commissioner without pay. Just at that time, a thought came to mind to go and live with the Paramount Chief's clerk so I could learn how to be a chief clerk. I

John Nimley Wulu, Sr., AA,BA

reasoned that if I become a clerk for the Paramount Chief, I wouldn't have to be a laborer. I asked a friend, "What do I need to do to become a Paramount Chief's clerk"? He said, "Go to school."

I believe it was the Lord who put that thought in my mind to ask the question, because of the prayer I did on my way back from Sinoe County, when I knelt and asked the Lord to show me which way to go and what to do so I wouldn't be a laborer or porter anymore.

But I still had a dilemma. In order for me to live with the Paramount Chief's clerk, my family would have to take me. It was our custom that before a child could move in and live with an adult other than a family member, the child's parents would have to take him to the adult's house and ask the adult's permission for the child to live with him or her. I knew if I went back to my town, there was a possibility that I could be sent out to do labor work. So I decided not to go back to Say-you-o.

That entire day I stayed in the house of a Towarbo man named Younwal Wisseh, the messenger to the Commissioner, thinking on what to do. Another thought came to my mind to go and live with a Mandingo man in the area, but I said no to that thought. Just at that time, one of the boys, named Jack Waylee, who worked with me at the Commissioner's compound and also came from the Towarbo Chiefdom, came in and we began a conversation. As we were talking, a thought came to mind about living at the mission (the missionaries' compound). I said to the boy, "I heard there is a mission around here, in Zwedru."

He answered, "Yes, there is a mission here. Look under the palm trees. Those are the missionaries' houses."

I saw some big white houses. I asked him to take me there. He agreed and I followed him to the mission. The mission was fenced in, but the gate was opened and we entered. We approached Reverend and Mrs. Jensen, who were sitting on the porch and asked us, "What do you want?"

I answered and said, "I want to live here and attend school."

14

The Miracles and Riches of God

They told us to come closer. Then the two of them put their heads together and talked. One of them asked me, "Where are you from?"

I responded, "I am from the Towarbo Chiefdom."

They put their heads together again and talked. I heard them say, "Let us take him to interpret for us when we go to his village to preach." And one of them asked, "Can you understand English?"

I answered, "I can understand and speak little bit of English." I believe the Lord was preparing me for this moment when He allowed my uncle Taley to take me to the Firestone plantation for those few months after my mother's death so I could learn a little bit of English. God is good. After letting them know that I could speak some English, they were convinced and agreed to take me on their mission to live. On Saturday evening, March 18, 1945, I moved onto the Assembly of God mission and started my new life. While I and the friend who took me to the mission were still standing before Rev. Jensen, he called one of the mission boys by the name of Paul Thomas and told him to take me to the boys' house.

Rev. Jensen gave me an empty cup and said, "When the food is cooked at the boys' house, the cooks will put your food in this cup. On Monday, you are to cut a bunch of palm nuts and bring them to us as payment for the empty cup." This was on Saturday. There were plenty of palm trees around the mission houses. A person could stand on the ground and cut a bunch of palm nuts.

The day the missionaries accepted me to live on their mission was the happiest day of my life. My friend who took me at the mission said to me, "Let us go back to the house. And spend the night, then you can come back tomorrow."

I told him, "I will sleep at the mission tonight and tomorrow. I will come and get my white bed sheet and my trousers." So he left me and went back to the house where we were lodging in the town. I followed Paul Thomas to the boys' house to start my new life at the mission. That night I was more than pleased. When we got to the boys' house, I

15

was just looking at the boys as they were moving about in front of the boys' house.

When it was time to go to bed, the boy who was in charge of all the boys asked me my name. I told him John and he said to follow him. He showed me a bamboo-and-wood bed stuffed with straw for me to sleep on. There was no mattress on the bed. At the time I had no idea of what a mattress was. I was just too happy to be at the mission. Saturday night, March 18, 1945, was the first night I slept at the mission in Tchien.

On Sunday morning, I went with the mission boys to church. This was my first time ever attending church. I was looking at the people in the church, admiring them as they sang God's songs. The minister talked about God. When church was over, I followed the boys back to the boys' house.

Later on that afternoon, I went to the house in Zwedru to get my bed sheet and trousers. When I got there, I told my laborer friends who were about to return to their towns that I was not going along with them to the Towarbo Chiefdom and that I was now staying at the mission to attend school.

With happiness in my heart, I informed my laborer friends to tell my townspeople that I would not be returning to Say-you-o. "The missionaries have accepted me at their mission. I am now staying at the mission. I am learning to be a Paramount Chief's clerk."

At that time, the Towarbo people had their own Paramount Chief, named Younmar, and one day I thought I could be the clerk to the chief. My friend laughed at me, making fun, saying things like, "As old as you are, what will you look like sitting in the class with infant readers learning the alphabets?" But with joy in my heart, I returned to the mission.

Early in the morning of March 20, 1945, I went along with the mission boys to Rev. Jensen so he could tell us what each of us would be doing from 8:00 a.m. to 12:00 noon each day during the week. My assignment, along with some other boys, was to clean around the

16

missionaries' houses cutting the grass. At noon I heard the bell ring and asked the boys I was working with what the bell was for. I was told that it was time for us to stop working and go to the boys' house to eat and get ready for school.

I was so happy that I was about to start my schooling that Monday afternoon. So I followed the boys to the boys' house. After eating, at 12:30, I saw many of the boys washing their faces and feet. I saw them greasing their faces and feet and brushing their hair. I was observing everything they were doing. So I followed suit and did everything I saw them doing.

At 1:00, the bell rang and it was school time. I saw all the boys going toward the church building, which was also the schoolhouse, and I followed them. As a new boy at the mission and on my first day in school, I did not know what to do. Other students were moving their chairs or benches closer toward the teacher. I did not know any of the teachers, so I just sat still. Then one of the missionaries said to us who were sitting, "Let all beginners or ABC students follow me outside, behind the church." I saw some children get up and follow her, so I followed also.

I did not know the ABCs, as the alphabet was called. And I was not in any grade or class. I was the oldest and tallest boy among the children in the ABC class. I was so anxious and eager to learn that I stood in front of the children in our beginner's class, but the missionary teacher, Miss LePeirce, held my hand, moved me from in front of the children, and said, "You are the biggest, tallest, and oldest boy in the ABC class. You must stand behind the children." I obeyed and started learning my ABCs on that day.

As a person with a strong determination and ambition to learn, I paid close attention to Miss LePeirce as she pronounced the letters of the alphabet. We repeated each letter after her. During the first semester, from March 20, 1945, to July 14, 1945, I memorized the entire alphabet

John Nimley Wulu, Sr., AA, BA

and could recite each letter by heart. I gave God the glory and praise for the golden opportunity he had given me to learn.

On July 15, 1945, school closed for the semester. We had two weeks break. Other students went home on vacation to see their parents. As for me, I wanted to continue in school throughout July. I had just been at the mission for three months and twenty-eight days and was not dreaming about going home at all.

In the first week of August 1945, the second-semester classes resumed. I was very happy to be in school because I knew the entire alphabet and could identify each letter. I was told I would be promoted to the Primer 1 class. On the first day of school, I was given a Primer 1 book to use in my class, which brought great joy to my heart.

It was just to my taste that I had my own Primer 1 book to study day and night. I give God all glory for giving me the intelligence to obtain knowledge for a better future.

During the second semester, I studied very hard. I was able to read through the Primer 1 and Primer 11 books before school closed on December 15, 1945. I was promoted to the Infant Reader by the end of the school year.

My promotion to the Infant Reader certainly brought great joy and happiness to my heart because within the period of eight months and twenty-nine days of being at the mission, I had completed the alphabet, Primer 1, and Primer II, and now I was going to begin the Infant Reader.

School was now closed, and some of the students were going on vacation to see their parents and relatives in the various towns. I was not ready to take a vacation yet. Then a good thought came to mind to stay at the mission during the two and a half months to study the Infant Reader. That sounded like a good idea to me. I said to myself, "I will study and go through the book before school opens." So I did not ask the missionaries concerning taking a vacation because I had decided to stay at the mission and study my Infant Reader.

18

The Miracles and Riches of God

During the first and second semesters, I made friends with the students who had completed the first and second grades. They were very young and were not my age, but I noticed that they were above me in grade. I became very friendly with those children. I made it a habit to share my food with them because I wanted them to help me with my lesson. They helped me pronounce words I could not pronounce and taught me the meanings of words I could not understand.

Every morning we would go to the church to pray. I made it my business to put my Infant Reader in my pocket, taking it everywhere I went. On our way back from church, I often found a chance to ask a student to pronounce one or two words for me before reaching the boys' house. I prayed and asked God to help me learn and know all the words in my Infant Reader before the school year began.

I had seventy-five days before school began, so I made it my business to read and study two to three pages in my reader every day. I also studied the spelling words that were at the back of the Infant Reader. I studied my multiplication (times table) and arithmetic, 1 + 1, 2 + 2, 3 + 3, 4 + 4, etc. Most of the arithmetic problems, I had already learned in the Primer I and II, so this was a review for me. I already knew my numbers from 1 to 100.

I really enjoyed the vacation because I was privileged to study my reader in the morning, afternoon, and evening by the blessed mercy and power of Almighty God. I gave God the glory for giving me the strength to study. It was He who gave me the ability to read through my Infant Reader within the space of two and a half months. All praise be to God.

It was March 1946, and school was about to open. I had planned not to take the Infant Reader when the semester began, but instead I would start the year in the first grade. But in order for me to do that, I would have to take the Infant Reader exam and pass it before I could be placed in the first grade class. I was ready, because I had been studying and preparing myself for the test all during the school break. The first

19

John Nimley Wulu, Sr., AA,BA

day of school, I told Mr. Wilson, my principal, "I will be taking the first grade class this semester and not the Infant Reader class because over the vacation break I studied the entire Infant Reader and know everything in it."

He said, "Okay, John, but I will have to test you to see if you really know everything in the Infant Reader."

The next day, the principal called me into his office and said, "Are you ready to take the exam?"

I said, "Yes, I am ready."

He said, "You are going to do reading, spelling, multiplication table, and arithmetic. Take one of the Infant Readers from among the books on the table and please listen and do exactly as I tell you." Then he said, "Open the book to page one and read until I tell you to stop." I opened the book to page one and started reading. I read more than ten pages, and then he told me to stop. He told me to open the book to the center of the book and start reading. I did and read a few more pages and he told me to stop. Then he told me to go toward the end of the book and start reading; I did, and I read to the end of the book. He said to me, "Yes, you can read the Infant Reader. Now it's time for the spelling and the multiplication table test." The principal turned to the back of the book he had in his hand to the page that listed the spelling words. He called out the words, and I spelled each one orally. I saw him smiling as he said that it was time for me to do the times tables. I recited the entire multiplication table from two to twelve.

In my heart I was thanking God for helping me do well on the test. When I looked, Principal Wilson was reclining in his chair and told me to get ready for an oral arithmetic test. He began to give me problems like $4 + 5, 6 + 6, 8 + 9, 10 + 5, 9 - 5, 10 - 6$; simple arithmetic problems. I solved all the problems correctly. At the end of the test, he looked at me and said, "John, you have passed the test. You do fit the first grade. You will get your first grade book tomorrow, and you will begin the first grade class."

The Miracles and Riches of God

I was very, very happy when Mr. Wilson informed me that I passed the test and I would be in the first grade class that semester. It was just to my taste because God had given me my desire. I was very grateful and thankful to God for the strength and good brains he had given me.

I did express my special thanks to the young children who assisted me greatly during the two months and fifteen days of school vacation. Sammy Graw and Peter Nyazee were some of the young children who assisted me with my lesson.

On the third day of class, a first grade book was issued to me. I took it to school and joined the first grade class. I was very pleased to be in the first grade. I paid close attention to the teacher in my class. During the first week of class, the teacher called on various students to read aloud in front of the class, but he did not call on me. I used that opportunity to study even harder because I knew he would be calling on me anytime.

In the second week, the teacher began calling on me to read the lesson. I felt recognized by the teacher. I was the only older boy in the class. All of the students were around nine or ten years of age. I started thinking again of what to do, so that I could be moved from among those young children. So I thought to myself that the best thing for me to do was to pray to God to give me the strength I needed to study hard, reading through the first grade book, learning all the spelling words, and knowing all the arithmetic before the first semester came to an end.

This way I could do what I'd done with the Infant Reader. At the beginning of the second semester, I could test out of the first grade class and get promoted to the second grade. And then I could leave the young first grade students behind.

I knew that in order for this to be accomplished, I must be the number one reader and the top in the class. I must know all the words in the first grade book and be able to spell each word from memory. I kept this thought to myself, it was my little secret. Everywhere I went,

21

John Nimley Wulu, Sr., AA,BA

my first grade book was in my pocket. I became very friendly with the young students who were above me in grade. I made sure to share my food with them because I needed their help.

It is very important that if any person wants to reach his desired goal, he must first seek God in a sincere prayer. He must not have evil intentions. Because of my sincere prayer, because of my strong trust and belief in God's mercy and great power, God gave me my heart's desire. At the end of the first semester, I was promoted to the second grade and was able to leave the young students behind in the first grade. I caught up with Yancy Peter Flah, Sammy Graw, and Peter Nyazee in the second grade.

It was a great joy in my heart when I got promoted to the second grade. At the beginning of the second semester, the second grade books were issued to me. I started studying hard again, just as I had with the Infant Reader and the first grade. My goal was to be promoted to the third grade by the end of the second semester, December 1946. And I did; I made double promotion in one year.

While I was at the mission, I also studied the Bible, the Word of God. The Bible was the number one important subject at the mission. I observed that the missionaries were in Liberia purposely to teach the Word of God, to preach and share the Gospel, the Good News of Jesus Christ, to us. The missionaries taught us the Bible. They told us to believe on the Lord Jesus Christ and we would be saved. So I believed in Jesus Christ and I am saved. One of the main verses I learned at the mission was John 3:16: "For God so loved the world that he gave his only begotten son, that whosoever believeth in him should not perish, but have everlasting life."

Rev. and Mrs. Jensen began to take me on preaching trips. Our preaching trips to Towarbo Chiefdom were very successful. We went to Say-you-o Town, my hometown, to preach the Gospel of Jesus Christ to my people. I was the interpreter for Rev. and Mrs. Jensen when they preached the Word of God. Their main purpose for taking me

22

The Miracles and Riches of God

with them was for me to interpret their words in my language to my people when they preached. Their purpose was fulfilled because each time they preached to my people, I interpreted for them. I also traveled with Rev. Jensen and his wife to Newarken Mission, Barrobo Chiefdom, and Maryland County in Liberia, West Africa, for the Christmas celebration. We had a wonderful and blessed time. I received my baptism at Newarken Mission in Barrobo Chiefdom.

Rev. and Mrs. Jensen were good and kind missionaries. They were very good to me. They took me on various preaching trips. They even took me to Tappeta Mission, where they printed booklets in the Tchien dialect. Rev. Jensen and his wife liked me because I was one of the good mission boys that obeyed the mission rules. Another reason why they took a liking to me was that they considered me to be a very brilliant person because of my outstanding grades in school. I made double promotion in one year, and on several occasions my name was posted on the honor roll board in the school.

It is very obvious that no one knows the future, only our blessed and merciful God of our Lord Jesus Christ knows. One day, I was at the mission, studying my third grade lesson, when a young man by the name of Youlo Blae came to me from Say-you-o Town and said to me, "John, you have to go with me to Say-you-o, your father has died." It was a great shock to me. I never dreamed of such bad news. I was very sad and started shedding tears. I did not know what to do when I heard that my father, Kayor Nie, had died.

With such great sorrow in my heart, I informed Rev. and Mrs. Jensen about the news of my father's death. I asked permission to go home to my father's funeral. They granted me authorization to go home with Youlo Blae, the young man who delivered the news of my father's death.

When I got in Say-you-o Town, my people saw me and started crying.

John Nimley Wulu, Sr., AA,BA

I joined them and began crying also. After crying for about an hour, my family comforted me and relayed to me how my father got sick and died. It was a very difficult time for me. When I got home, the family had already buried my father. It was indeed a very sad and unhappy occasion. I was really hurt because I did not get to view my father's body.

In my custom, when a parent dies, after the burial, a date is set for the family to hold special ceremonies that could last for weeks. During the ceremonies, large feasts are held with lots of foods. Cows, goats, and chickens are killed and cooked in various kinds of sauces. Side dishes such as rice, plantains, cassava roots, and corn are prepared.

The ceremonies lasted for a few weeks. So I stayed in my town with my family until the ceremonies were over. When the ceremonies were over, I went back to Tchien mission. The missionaries were pleased and welcomed me back with appreciation. And I was very pleased that they accepted me back on campus.

The school year began in March 1947. I was in the third grade. I was very glad to be back in school and planned to study hard again. At the end of 1947, I was promoted to the fourth grade. In 1948 I went through the fourth grade; at the end of that year, December, I was promoted to the fifth grade. It was a blessing for me to live at the mission with missionaries who were very kind to me. I really enjoyed the mission life. It was at the mission I learned the Word of God and became a Christian. The missionaries always encouraged me to study the Word of God. I am very grateful for my mission experience.

My Son Caesar-Francois Wulu

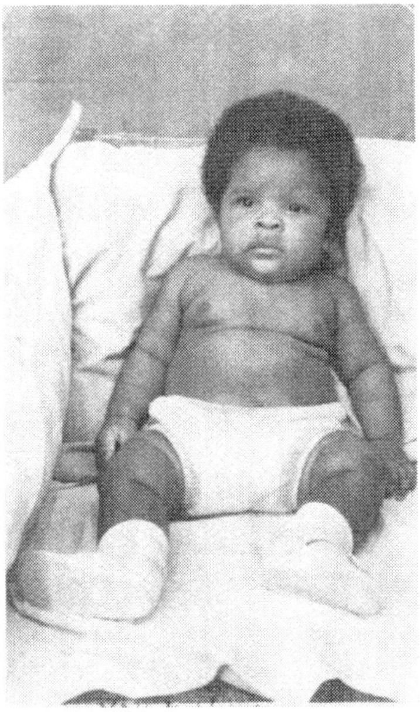

Kaller-Minnie Yah Wulu, our seventh child

I am getting out of my car

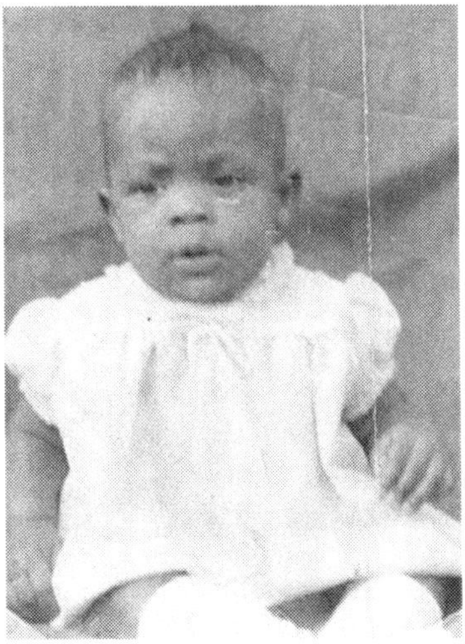

Johnnette P. Wulu, our ninth child

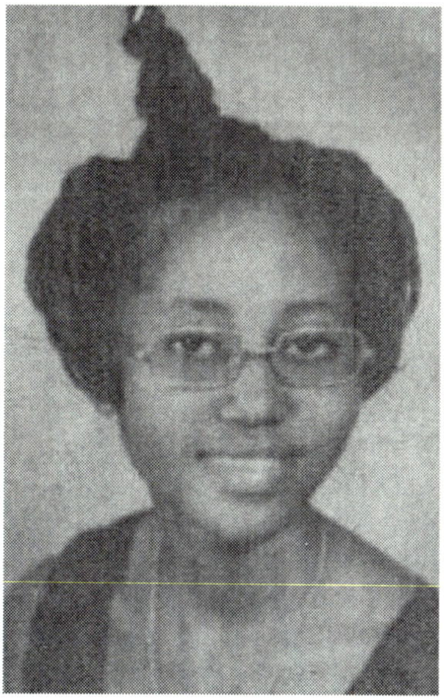

My Daughter, Elizabeth Wulu

*Emmanuel's high school graduation:
left to right - Solomon, Papa Wulu,
Francois-Caesar, Emmanuel, Mommy,
John Jr., Kaller, Johnnette and Aaron*

Students of our school in Monrovia, John Wulu Elementary School

Mommy and myself with teachers and students at our school

I am with the students and teachers at my school in Monrovia, Liberia

My school, Richard M. Nixon Institute, Gala Day parade

Papa Wulu

Judydi and her daughter

My grandson, Timothy with his mother Rose

CHAPTER 3
ANOTHER UNEXPECTED BLESSING: LIFE IN MONROVIA

In March 1949, Rev. Jensen and his wife informed me that they were about to go on vacation. They were going back to the United States, but they were not leaving me on the Tchien mission. They would send me to Cape Palmas, Maryland County, to live with some missionaries and continue my schooling. But after a day or two, Mrs. Jensen called me and asked if I would like to go to Monrovia, the capital city of Liberia, to live with some missionaries there and attend school. I told her yes.

I was very, very happy that the Lord had shown great kindness to me. He brought me from my village, not knowing where to go. He put me at the mission and gave me great missionaries to live with, who taught me God's Word, and I became a Christian. I attended school living at the mission. Now He was opening another door for me to go to Monrovia, the capital city, to live with missionaries and continue my education on a higher level. I will forever praise the Lord.

On March 12, 1949, we left Tchien Mission, Zwedru, Eastern Province, and now Grand Gedeh County. We walked four days on foot to Tappeta, Center Province, now Nimba County. At the time when I was at the mission, there were no cars traveling from Tchien to Tappeta because we had no roads or streets in that area.

29

John Nimley Wulu, Sr., AA,BA

We reached Tappeta Mission on the evening of March 16. It was still daylight. We spent the night at Tappeta Mission. On the 17th of March 1949, Rev. and Mrs. Jensen were able to get a passenger car for us to travel to Monrovia. We left Tappeta Mission in the afternoon for Monrovia. This was my first time ever riding in a passenger car and my first time ever traveling such long distance of some three hundred or more miles in a passenger car. The car was an old passenger truck. The road was not paved, and there were chuckholes in it. The truck was bouncing all over the road. Within three to four hours of riding, I began vomiting in the truck and feeling sick. We arrived in Monrovia on March 18, 1949, early in the morning.

I was very, very happy that we reached our destination, Monrovia, Liberia. When I got out of the truck, all of my body, my hair, and clothes were covered with dust, but I did not consider it to be anything at all. I was too glad that I was in Monrovia, our capital city. Rev. and Mrs. Jensen had brought me to Monrovia as they had promised when we were at the Tchien mission.

I was very grateful to the Lord God of Jesus Christ. It was a great joy in my heart as I was moving to the back yard of the missionary's house, where I was going to live and attend school. As we were in the back yard, Rev. John Hurston came to the back door, greeted Rev. and Mrs. Jensen, and asked them to come into the house.

I helped to take their luggage inside. Within less than an hour, Rev. Jensen had introduced me to Rev. and Mrs. John Hurston. They told them that I was a good boy and that they'd brought me along to live with them and attend school. They also told Rev. and Mrs. Huston that I was a brilliant and obedient boy. Rev. and Mrs. Hurston were pleased and they accepted me to live with them.

Mrs. Hurston took Mrs. Jensen into the guest room, and I carried their luggage. Afterward, Mrs. Hurston took me to the back room in the same house and told me that this was my room. I believe the room

30

was about 12 by 7 feet in size. I was very pleased and happy because I had been accepted and had a room of my own to live in.

Mrs. Hurston also showed me the kitchen area where I would do my cooking, and she showed me my bathroom. Everything was beautiful, and I believe that God had made it possible for me to be in Monrovia, the capital city. I gave all praise and glory to God.

In the evening, I went to bed and slept well. The next morning, I got up and went in my bathroom, brushed my teeth, washed my face, went back to my room, and greased my face real good. And then I went in the house to say good morning to Rev. Jensen and his wife. I also said good morning to Rev. John Hurston and his wife, the missionaries I would be living with in Monrovia. When I came out of the house, later on that morning, Mrs. Hurston called me and showed me the work I would be doing in the house every morning before going to school in the afternoon.

My job was to go in the various bedrooms in the house while the missionaries were having breakfast and make up the beds, sweep every room, and dust the tables and chairs. It was also my duty to clean the living room, dust the chairs and table, clean the hallways, and get the beds ready in the evening for sleeping, and I was to also clean the yard.

During the first two weeks, I did my work according to the instructions I had received from my boss lady. Everything was okay with me because the assignment was good for me. My boss lady told me that I was doing a good job.

In the first week of April 1949, my boss lady told me to go and register at one of the afternoon schools in the area. I was very pleased. So the following day, I went and registered at J. B. McCrithy Afternoon School. I started attending school in the afternoon with no embarrassment in my studies at all. I took the fifth grade. The class work was very easy for me because I did a lot of studying during the school vacation. I was very happy that I was in school.

John Nimley Wulu, Sr., AA,BA

As a newcomer in the capital city, I saw many things in the city that were not at the Tchien mission. I saw paved streets in Monrovia; cars in the streets and people driving them all around the city. Monrovia had electricity. Some of the streets had streetlights. Some homes had electric lights. Monrovia also had running water. We got water from the faucet. During my first fifteen years in Monrovia, the Executive Mansion, our president's dwelling place, was on Ashmun Street, the same street my missionary's house was on. From our house to the Executive Mansion was only three or four minutes' walk.

When I was at Tchien Mission, we did not have running water, electric lights, paved streets, or cars, nor was there anyone driving cars on the dusty roads. As I was making comparisons with things in Monrovia and at the Tchien mission, I did not forget my studies in school. At the end of the school year, December 15, 1949, I was promoted to the six grade. During the vacation, I bought some sixth-grade books and studied as hard as I had at the Tchien mission in Zwedru.

At the beginning of 1950, J. B. McCrithy School closed down. The owner of the building requested it. So those of us who were attending the school were compelled to search for another one. It is good to put your trust in God. I had a belief that the Lord would open a way for me to attend a good school. So I began to pray, asking the Lord to lead me to a good school. It is obvious that prayer is the key that opens heaven's door. I prayed, and God made a way for me.

In the latter part of February 1950, I was told that the Laboratory High School had a junior high section with seventh and eighth grades. So I went to the school to find out whether this was true. The registrar confirmed that they did have seventh- and eighth-grade classes. So for the next three weeks, I could hardly sleep. I spent time studying sixth-grade arithmetic, English, and spelling. I had planned to take the seventh-grade class. But I also knew I would be tested on the sixth-grade subjects, so I prepared myself by studying for the test.

The Miracles and Riches of God

At the time I was trying to enroll in the Laboratory High School, I realized that the school was a long walking distance from my house. The school was meeting at the University of Liberia, but at that time, the distance was no problem to me. My concern was passing the test so I could take the seventh-grade class.

In the first week in March 1950, Laboratory High School announced that a test would be given that next week to new students entering the seventh, eighth, and ninth grades. That was just to my taste because that gave me more time to study my arithmetic, English, and spelling. I was praying and studying because I was determined to pass the test. It is my belief that with God all things are possible.

On the morning of the second Friday in March 1950, I went to Laboratory High School and joined other students to take the test, but before going I prayed and asked God to give me a good understanding of the test. I went to the school and took the test. We were told to come back on Tuesday the following week to check the bulletin board for the test results. I went home and started praying again because I learned from the Bible that Jesus says if we ask anything from the father in His name, we will receive what we ask for. I have faith in the Word of God, so I believed that the Lord had shown me the right way to take the test.

It pays to have faith in the Word of God. In the New Testament, Hebrews 11:1 says, "Now faith is the substance of things hoped for, the evidence of things not seen." Verse 3 says, "Through faith we understand that the world was framed by the Word of God, so that things which are seen were not made of things which do appear." Verse 7 says, "By faith Noah, being warned of God of things not seen as yet, moved with fear, prepared an ark to the saving of his house; by which he condemned the world, and became heir of the righteousness which is by faith."

Having faith in the blessing power of God and a firm belief that I had passed the test, I went to Laboratory High School right after I completed my morning assignment on Tuesday. When I got to the

33

John Nimley Wulu, Sr., AA,BA

school, I headed directly to the bulletin board to see the test results. I looked on the board and saw my name under grade seven. I was very happy and thanked God for answering my prayers.

With happiness in my heart as a seventh-grade student, I went to the school bookstore and purchased my seventh-grade books. I went home, took my books to my room, and began studying them. I was so pleased that I passed my test. On Thursday of that same week I started the seventh grade at Laboratory High School. I walked thirty-five minutes each way every day to school.

All the teachers in our junior high division were good in their various subjects. But I really enjoyed our math teacher, Mr. Timothy Yarn. He was very good in math. His teaching method was very clear. I gained more knowledge in my seventh- and eighth-grade math classes in the junior high division under Professor Yarn than I had in other classes. I thank God for him.

In 1950 and 1951 I went through the seventh and eighth grades. At the end of 1951, I was promoted to the ninth grade. I gave Almighty God praise for my promotion. I believe I was able to get this far because of my strong determination and ambition with confidence in the Word of God.

After my promotion to the ninth grade, I began to consider the long walking distance to and from Laboratory High School. I started thinking about what school I could attend for the ninth grade. Laboratory offered ninth grade, but the distance was getting to be a problem. Then the thought came to me, "Pray, and put the problem before God. He will show you the right high school to attend." So I started praying to the Lord. In February 1952, the missionary I lived with told me that it would be better for me to attend a Christian school. He said, "It will be good for you to register at the College of West Africa, on Ashmun Street near us. It is just two to three minutes' walking distance."

The College of West Africa was a Christian institution. American missionaries and leaders of the Methodist church who had come to

The Miracles and Riches of God

Liberia in the early 1900s established the school. The College of West Africa was a high school. One of its main and very important subjects was the Bible. I was very happy and pleased when my missionaries encouraged me to attend a Christian institution, and one that was near us, on the same street as our house.

My boss lady told me I could attend school in the morning because the College of West Africa high school had only morning section. The tuition was only $9 per semester.

I was now a high school student. I had a new boss lady, who gave me new assignments. My job was to wash the clothes and iron them. I was very pleased with my job. My new boss lady was Miss Mary Martin, a missionary from the state of Maryland, USA.

I purchased my ninth-grade books and starting attending classes the last week of February 1952. It was a short walking distance for me. It pays to pray, put your trust in God, and have faith in him. The College of West Africa was one of the best high schools in Liberia at the time. The Lord made it possible for me to attend a very good Christian school. I am thankful to Christ Jesus for giving me such a good opportunity.

The president of the College of West Africa was a good Christian missionary named Mr. Carey. Although he was the president, he still taught the Bible at the school.

When I was a young man living at the mission, I was very attracted to females, because I kept myself very clean and well dressed. Some females would tell me, "John, you are a very good looking young man and you dress well." There are problems everywhere. In this world, only the great God knows what is good for every person. I endeavored my best not to be influenced by sweet talk or kind words said about me by some females. But on this particular day, a man by the name of Steven, a cook for the missionaries, invited me to his house. He lived outside of the Assembly of God mission, founded by Miss Martin in the Brewerville area in Liberia.

John Nimley Wulu, Sr., AA,BA

I went to visit Mr. Steven at his house. After having a good conversation for about an hour, Mr. Steven said, "Let's take a walk to my neighbor's home." I agreed and we walked to his neighbor's. His neighbor's name was Agnes. She was busy at the back of her house. So we moved closer to her. Steven said, "Miss Agnes, how are you doing?"

She said, "I am doing fine, Steven. Steven, who is this young fellow?" Steven said, "I am sorry, I should have introduced my good and fine friend to you in the first place. Miss Agnes, this is John Nimley Wulu. John, this is Miss Agnes, a pretty lady and good neighbor." She came closer to me and I moved toward her. She shook my hand smiling and I smiled also.

"Are you living here in Brewerville?" she asked.

"I am staying with missionaries in Monrovia. I am attending the College of West Africa in Monrovia, but I am spending my vacation on the new Assembly of God mission around here in your area. When school is opened, I will go back to Monrovia to attend school."

"You are welcome to our neighborhood," she said.

"Thank you, fine lady," I remarked. Then, we left and I went back to the mission.

After a week, Steven told me that his good neighbor lady asked about me and said good things about me. I asked him, "Who is your good neighbor lady?"

"The lady whose home I took you to—Miss Agnes," he said.

I then told Steven, "Okay, if it will not be a problem, I will pay her a visit, since she said nice things about me. I am attracted to her."

The following week, I started visiting Miss Agnes. Each time I visited her, she spoke to me nicely. Our friendship grew stronger and stronger. Shortly after that, we had my first child. I was still in high school. My first beautiful child's name is Elizabeth; her mother is Miss Agnes Banks, who was a good lady who did not trouble me about my child.

36

The Miracles and Riches of God

After my daughter was born, some friends said to me, "Your school business will be messed up because you have a child."

I told them, "God knows what is best for me, and I will accept what is best for me. I will pray and ask God to help me to continue my schooling. The Lord who made a way for me to go to the mission and made it possible for me to be in high school will surely help me continue my education."

So, I started praying to God. I said, "Lord, help me to continue my schooling. Friends are telling me that my school situation will be messed up because I have a child. You are the one who made it possible for the child to come into the world. Without your assistance, I will not reach my goal. With you, all things are possible. I believe you, Lord, because of all you have done for me because I have prayed."

I am telling my story about my experience while coming up as a young man because every young person will face some type of attraction in life. But whenever you have a problem, always put your problem before God. He is ready at any time to answer your sincere and faithful prayer. As a young person, always think twice and exercise self-control in everything you do.

Elizabeth on visit to Liberia listening to family members

My first two sons, Emmanuel and John Jr., high school graduation picture

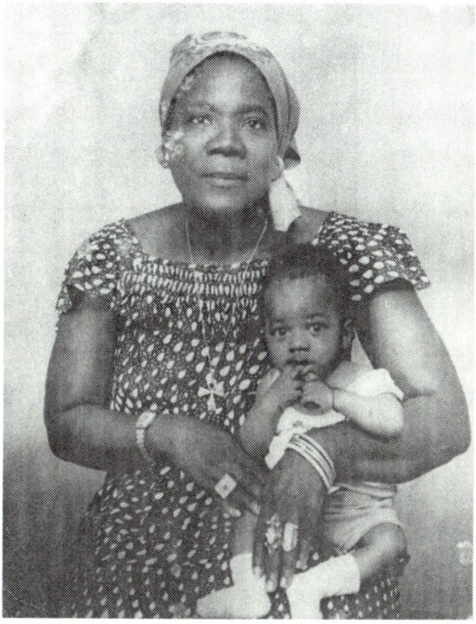

Mommy holding one of our grandchildren

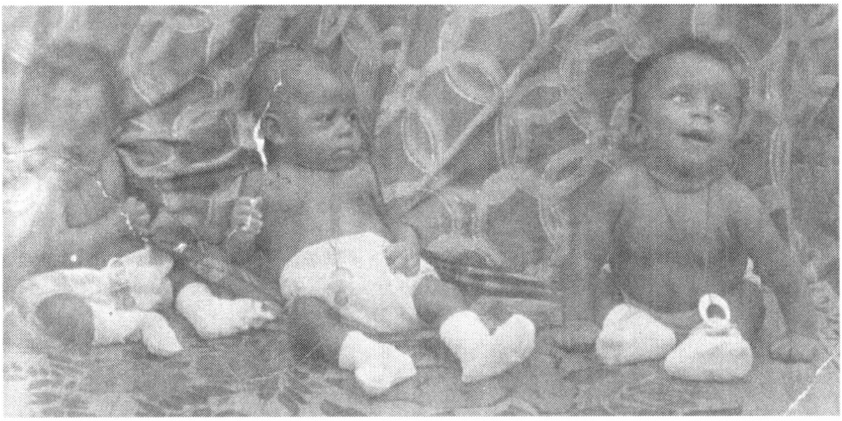

Emmanuel's children: Taenoomu, Emmilk, and Darlington Wulu

Mommy and myself with teachers from our school.

Mr. Wulu, Sr. and his employees at Unity Conference Center

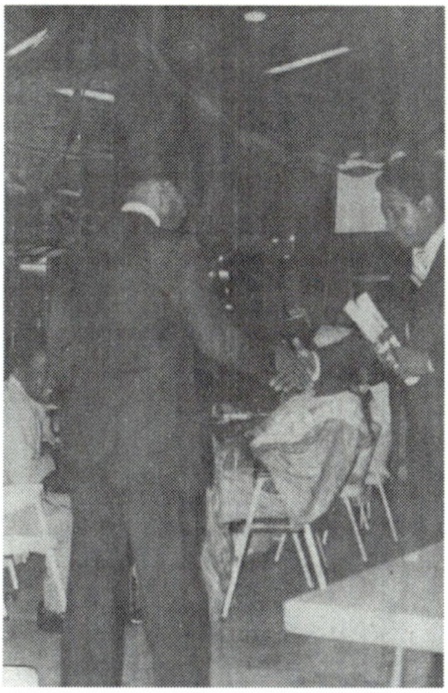

Hon. John N. Wulu, Sr. receives award for establishing schools in Monrovia from Deputy Minister Duncun of Education

My grandchildren, Musa and Otis

I received a certificate from Affinity Missionary Baptist Church School.

I posed for a picture after the presentation.

My second high school building, Richard M. Nixon Institute, named after the President of the United States

Richard M. Nixon Institute Gala Anniversary celebration 2001-2002

I am talking with one of my friends at a party

ABOVE: Mommy took picture with Richard M. Nixon teachers and students

LEFT: Elizabeth visits Papa and Mommy's school. Left to right: Elizabeth, Mother Mary, Mama Agnes Banks and Sarah

Left to right: Hon. John N. Wulu, Sr., Assistant Minister Teeklo

Executive Director of Unity Conference Center, John N. Wulu, Sr. and his security, Mr. Doe

CHAPTER 4
MY LOVE, THE LONG HAIR BEAUTY

With strong determination, ambition, and prayer, I continued my education. December of 1954, I was promoted to the twelfth grade. I was very happy that I got promoted. My school business was not messed up, because God answers prayer. Within the space of three years, I completed the ninth, tenth, and eleventh grades and was promoted to the twelfth.

School was closed for two months and a half. During the vacation, I went to spend time with my cousin Fineboy at Bishop Brook, near Bassa Community in Monrovia. While I was standing outside of my cousin's house, I saw an attractive, pretty, beautiful, good-looking girl with long hair and fat legs going to her friend's house. It was in the evening. Later on, the two of them came outside and were standing and talking. I moved toward them to picture the girl I saw with my two eyes to make sure that my eyes did not deceive me.

After she left her friend's house, I went to her friend and asked her who the girl was. She said, "Her name is Minnie Kyne. She is from Pleebo, Maryland County."

"Could you please tell me your name?" I asked.

"My name is Beatrice," she said.

I said, "I would like to talk with your friend the next time she comes over."

John Nimley Wulu, Sr., AA,BA

Beatrice asked, "Why do you want to talk to her?"

I told her, "The girl is beautiful and very attractive. I would like to talk with her if you would permit me."

Luckily, one week later, one evening she went to visit Beatrice. I was sitting in a chair in front of my cousin Fineboy's house when I saw her coming out from her friend's house going home. I got up and tried to catch up with her, but I could not make it. I started thinking about the attractive girl. But I said to myself, "Exercise self-control concerning attraction. This is vacation, try to do what is right during this vacation. Be sure to use your head." Since I could not catch up with her, I went to Beatrice's house to ask her whether she had delivered my message to her friend. Beatrice said, "Yes, I told my friend that you wanted to talk with her." When I heard what Beatrice said, I was pleased that she had delivered my message to her friend.

For two weeks, I did not see the beautiful girl. I was trying to control myself. I did not go out too often. I was doing my studies because I desired greatly to graduate from high school in 1955. But only the great Lord knows the future of everyone in this wonderful world.

One day I got up feeling very good. I began to think about the long-haired girl. So I got a nice haircut, took a cool bath, and greased and combed my hair nicely. I put on my new, sharp-looking clothes and a nice pair of shoes. I wanted to be attractive to the pretty girl. In other words, I wanted to be admired or noticed by the fat-legged girl.

I was young and kept myself clean. I always put on clean and nice clothes that fitted me neatly, because on various occasions I had gotten compliments from girls as well and grown women, telling me that I looked good in my clothes.

After getting dressed, I decided to stroll around to Beatrice's house. As I was strolling there, luckily the beautiful girl who attracted me was coming directly my way. So I moved a little faster toward her and met her. I said to her, "Fine girl, how are you doing?"

The Miracles and Riches of God

She said, "I am doing okay." I held her hand and looked straight into her eyes smiling and she started smiling also.

I said within myself, This is the girl I saw twice. While looking at her from head to toe, I said to her, "Would you please walk with me for a few minutes? I would like to talk to you." She agreed. I asked her very politely if she knew a lady by the name of Beatrice. She answered, "Yes, she is my true friend."

"Has Beatrice told you anything concerning what a young fellow said to her?" I asked.

"Yes, she said. "Oh, you are the one Beatrice informed me about. Beatrice told me that one young, good-looking, and handsome fellow asked about me two times and wanted to talk with you." While she was talking, she looked at me up and down smiling, and I smiled too. She said, "My name is Minnie Kyne." I said, "My name is John."

I asked about her parents and where she was presently living. She said her parents were in Pleebo, Maryland County. She was living with Professor Moraia near Camp Johnson Road in Monrovia. I told her that I was living with missionaries on Ashmun Street near the Executive Mansion and that I was spending my vacation at my cousin Fineboy's home in Bishop Brook near Bassa Community.

As we were strolling, she said, "Why are you asking me all these questions?"

I said to her, "You are a fine and beautiful girl. Your beauty attracted me when I saw you talking to your friend. I have seen you twice, but I have not been privileged to talk to you. You have a fine face, long hair, fat legs, good hips, a slim body, and you are very attractive. I admired you."

She was smiling, holding my hand tightly, and said, "You are a fine and handsome fellow and very attractive also."

While I was smiling and holding her hand tightly, I said, "My main purpose for talking to you is that I want you to be my friend. I would like to visit you if you give me permission."

Then she said, "It is not bad to have a friend. You can visit me next Saturday afternoon." I said it would be between four and five o'clock in the afternoon.

While holding her hand, I went closer to her, put my left hand around her, kissed her on the check, and said to her, "Beauty, I will see you next week Saturday, by the help of God."

And she said, "It is a pleasure talking with you, fine fellow." I left her, she went her way, and I went home with joy and happiness in my heart. I was very pleased because I spoke with the girl.

The next Saturday, I went to her house on Camp Johnson Road to visit her. When I got in the area, I asked someone to direct me to Professor Moraia's house. The person took me in front of the house. I reached out and knocked on the door. A lady came to the door and asked me who I was. I told her my name was John and that I came to visit Miss Minnie Kyne.

The lady went back and called the fine girl. She came to the door, opened it for me, and said, "Come in." I did, and she kissed me on my cheek. She told some of her people in the house that I asked her to be my friend and promised to visit her. All of them were looking at me smiling. I usually dress to attract people. So when I saw them smiling, I said to myself, I look attractive to them. The pretty girl told me to sit down. So I did. After a few minutes, I told her I preferred to take our chairs outside under the trees and do our talking. She agreed, so we went outside and sat by ourselves. I said to her, "The last time, I told you that I wanted you to be my friend. I love you. You are a beautiful girl. If you like me and admire me deeply in your heart, I would like to inform your guardians about my desire before leaving."

She was smiling, looking straight in my face, and said, "I admire and love you too. You are a good-looking fellow. When you entered the house, all my people were looking at you. When I told them that you wanted to be my friend, they started smiling. I am sure they will like you."

The Miracles and Riches of God

After we had a conversation for about an hour or more, we went back in the house. She called her guardians' attention and told them that I wanted to talk with them. One of the ladies said, "Tell us, what do you want, young man?"

I told them, "I love your daughter and I want her to be my girlfriend."

One of the ladies said to me, "Thank you, young man. You have come here for a good purpose and we like what you told us."

Then the oldest lady said to the girl I liked, "Jel-la-yai [her nickname], do you like this boy. He seems to be a small boy. Do you think he will be able to help you?"

The girl answered, "Yes, he said he loves me and he wants me to be his girlfriend. I love him and want him to be my boyfriend also."

"Well, my good young man," the spokeslady said, "you love our daughter and our daughter loves you also. We love you, you are a fine person, and you are a good-looking fellow. You may visit our daughter anytime you want. Do not be afraid to come to our house from now on."

I answered, "Many thanks," got up, shook their hands, and said goodbye to them. My pretty girl walked with me outside. I told her to please expect me every weekend.

She thanked me and said, "You said good things to my people, they like you. I love you dearly and you are welcome anytime you want to see me." I got hold to her hand, pulled her closer to me, held her tightly, kissed her straight in her mouth for more than two minutes, and then released her. I looked straight in her eyes and said, "My beauty, you are for me and I am for you." I walked away from her and she went back into the house.

I went back home and into my room, knelt down, and started praying to the Lord. I asked him to help me and give me what was good for me because only he knew what was good for me in this wonderful world. It was the beginning of January 1955, seven more weeks before

John Nimley Wulu, Sr., AA, BA

school opened. So I got some of my twelfth-grade books and started reading and studying.

It really pays to think of what will benefit you in the future. So I said within myself, 'Education is the number one thing that is going to benefit me in the future. So let me read my English and history books, take notes, and study well.' I was also praying very hard so the Lord could help me graduate from high school at the end of that year.

I am very thankful to God that He gave me self-discipline and self-determination to always concentrate on beneficial things that would enable me to be self-reliant in the future. He always gave me the strength I needed to obtain sound and better education to help me get a better job.

It does not pay to do two things at the same time. So during the vacation, I visited my pretty girlfriend. I said to her, "For six good weeks we have seen one another, and school is about to reopen. I will not be able to visit you as regularly as I have, because I have to study hard to get out of high school this year."

School opened in the last week of February 1955. I started going to classes in the twelfth grade at the College of West Africa. I completed the first semester of my twelfth-grade class but had to drop out of school because of circumstances beyond my control. With firm determination, I did enroll at Martha Tubman Memorial Academy in the twelfth grade in 1956 and graduated the same year.

I was very, very happy when I received my high school diploma. I was very grateful and thankful to Almighty God, who had made it possible for me to go through high school. This is a matter of fact that when you put your trust in God and pray sincerely with faith for anything, He will surely give it to you.

I thank the Lord God for Rev. and Mrs. Jensen, who took me in at the Tchien mission in March 1945 in Zwedru, Tchien District, Eastern Province, now Grand Gedeh county, Liberia. I also thank God for Rev. Hurston and his kind wife for accepting me to live with them on the

48

The Miracles and Riches of God

Assembly of God mission in Monrovia when Rev. and Mrs. Jensen were traveling back to their home on vacation.

I give praise to our blessed God for Miss Mary Martin, a missionary in Liberia from the state of Maryland whom the Hurstons left me with when they were returning to the United States on a two to three years' leave of absence from the mission. She was very good and kind to me. On various occasions I traveled with her to the Barclay Training Center in Monrovia, where she preached the gospel message of Jesus Christ to the young people on Sunday afternoons.

She always gave me good advice. She told me to love the Lord Jesus Christ, do God's way, and don't forget to pray. It was sorrow and grief to my heart when she passed away at Barobo Newken Mission in Maryland County, Liberia. May her soul rest in peace.

After my graduation from high school, I decided to seek a job and work for a few years before going to college, because a college education was much more expensive than high school tuition. Even college books were costly.

While attending high school, I had not forgotten about getting some basic educational training skills that could land me a job. So I took up typing at a private school and attended evening classes. While attending typing classes, I did not forget to pray to the Lord to help me gain my typing skills. I knew that without any type of skills after graduating from high school, it would be very difficult for me to get a job. So I began preparing myself.

Keep it in mind that God is good. He will give you any good thing you pray for. While attending typing classes, the Lord made it possible for me to get a secondhand typewriter at a very low price. This was what I used to practice on at home. Remember that practice makes perfect. With God's help, I was able to type between twenty-five and thirty words per minute.

I also attended the College of West Africa business section in the afternoon, where I obtained a bookkeeping certificate. Mrs. Smith,

John Nimley Wulu, Sr., AA, BA

the head of the business section, who later became the president of the College of West Africa, taught me bookkeeping. It is very important to prepare yourself before getting out in the field to search for a job. It is very obvious that a better future awaits those who have good and productive educational skills.

At the beginning of the new year, January 1957, I was pleased that I had typing and bookkeeping skills plus my high school diploma. So I started going out to search for a job. I went to the Assembly of God mission school principal's office to apply. Miss Anna Staford was in charge of the afternoon section. She knew me. I was living with them at the mission. I served as a Sunday School teacher and also as a Sunday School superintendent in our church. I had experience in teaching children. Miss Staford said to me, "John, you are now a high school graduate and you have been dealing with children in our Sunday School. I believe you are able to teach the first grade class at the Assembly of God mission school afternoon section. If you are interested, I will employ you at the beginning of March this year to teach the first grade class." I was very happy when she told me that.

At the beginning of March, I was employed at the Assembly of God mission school afternoon section as a first-grade teacher. My starting salary was US$25 per month. I was very glad that my missionaries gave me a teaching job. I praised God for the job. It is really a matter of fact that when you are in need of anything and you pray and ask the Lord in faith, He will surely give it to you. I prayed to the Lord to make a way for me, and He provided a good job for me.

In August, the middle part of 1957, I was practicing on my typewriter for more speed when my former classmate, Joseph Toe, knocked at my door. I said, "Come in". He entered. I said to him, "Sit down Joe". He sat down and said to me, "John, are you looking for a job? "Yes", I said. "There is an open position for a clerk typist in my office. Prepare and come to take a typing test tomorrow," he said.

The Miracles and Riches of God

I was more than happy that my friend Joe informed me of the open position. I said in my heart that this was a blessed opportunity for me. I will not leave this typewriter until midnight. I had a twelfth-grade book of English literature in my room that I used to do all my typing practice.

With a strong desire to pass the test, I practiced typing from page to page until after midnight, then I went to bed. Very early in the morning, I got up and prayed. After praying, I went in the bathroom and brushed my teeth and washed my face and then went back in my room. I drew my chair up to the table with the typewriter and sat down. I bowed my head and prayed, "Lord, I am in your hands and I am doing the practice because I want the clerk job. So help me to pass the test and give me the clerk typist position, in Jesus' name. Amen."

Then I started typing from page to page in my English lit book. I typed many pages, for over three hours that morning. I then left the room and went to take a good bath. I returned; greased my skin, face, and hair; combed my hair real good; and put on my clothes, tie, and shoes. I knelt down and prayed to the Lord and asked Him to help me pass the test and give me the job. I got up, took my application, and stepped out of my room. I locked the door behind me and started my job-searching journey.

I took a taxi to the Monrovia Port Management Company office at the Freeport of Monrovia. When I got out of the taxi, I went in the office and gave my application to the office manager. After reading it over, he took me to the chief clerk to test me on the typing skills. People, God is good. He did a wonderful and great thing for me that day when I submitted my application for the clerk typist position, which I pray never to forget.

Mr. James Nabge, the chief clerk, showed me a desk with a typewriter on it and a chair to sit in to take the test. The chief clerk looked on his desk for the document for me to be tested on but could not find it.

But just to show the greatness and miraculous power of God, a clerk typist named Eugene Natt, working in the office but attending night school, had brought in his English literature book with him to work

John Nimley Wulu, Sr., AA,BA

on this particular day and had it on his desk. The chief clerk picked the book up from the typist's desk, gave it to me, and said, "Open the literature and use any page for your test."

At the time he handed me the book, I thought I was dreaming. But it was a real blessing and wonderful miracle of God because that book was the same type of English lit book that I did my practice on at home. So I put my head down and said, "Lord God, thank you for your great and wonderful power. You have given me the job."

Then I lifted up my head and drew the chair near to the desk. I placed my feet in the right order, opened the literature book the chief clerk handed me, and started typing from the first page in chapter one. After typing for more than five minutes, the manager came and took the test paper from the typewriter and took it to his office to review. A while later, he called me and said, "You have passed the test. You may come to work tomorrow." That was August 26, 1957.

I was very, very happy and I went and told the chief clerk, Mr. James Nagbe, that the manager told me that I passed the test and I must start work tomorrow. I left the office and went home with happiness. When I got home, I met my pretty and beautiful loved one sitting on the bed. With joy in my heart, I immediately informed her that I passed the test and that the office manager told me that I could come to work tomorrow. She was very, very pleased. She held my hand, hauled me to herself, and started kissing me in my mouth, on my cheek and face, and the both of us fell into bed and started thanking God for a job.

After praising God, I told her about the miracle that the great God had performed at the Port Management Company's office when I put in the application for the job, how one clerk who worked in the office and attended night school had taken his English lit book to the office and had it on his desk, and how the chief clerk picked up the literature from the clerk's desk and gave it to me to use to take the test and told me to use any page. The same type of literature I used to practice at home was given to me to use for the test.

52

The Miracles and Riches of God

When I got through talking about the Lord's miracle, she and I talked about how good God is and how He answers prayers when one puts one's trust and confidence in Him. I told my pretty girl that I now needed to rest. She said, "Yes, you need a good rest now while I prepare a good dinner for you. You have done remarkable through God's miracle. The Lord God is our director for the future."

While my long-haired girl was preparing dinner, I had two hours of sleep. After dinner was prepared, a table was set, and everything I needed was on it. My fine girl came and kissed me on my cheek and said, "Come, the food is ready." I got up and went into the bathroom, washed my mouth and hands, and joined her at the table. We said our grace and really enjoyed the food.

The following morning, I got up around 6:00 a.m. I went into the bathroom and brushed my teeth. I then took a warm bath and returned to my room and greased my hair and combed it nicely. I put on my clean clothes, tie, and shoes. My eyes were on the time clock because I wanted to be at the Monrovia Port Management Company on time. My beauty said, "Try to be on time always, because you are a new employee."

When I looked at my clock, it was 7:00 a.m. So I knelt down and prayed, "Lord God, I am now going to start the job you have given me. Be with me and let this job be a permanent position for me. Let it be a blessed one that my coming family, partner, and I will enjoy. I will give you praise. Give me strength and understanding of how to work in this world. May you direct my path always, in Christ's name I pray."

I got up and stepped out of the room, and my loved one locked the door behind me. I took a taxi to the Monrovia Port Management Company. If my mind serves me right, I was the first person to arrive at the office before the other employees. The chief clerk, Mr. Nagbe, showed me a desk with a typewriter on it and a chair and said, "This is your desk, on which you will do your work. You are welcome." That was the same desk I used to take my test.

53

Papa Wulu

Papa Wulu

*My brother and I, David Q. Nimley (third
from right) and his children*

My son, Aaron Wulu's children: left to right - Christopher, Avner, Aaron Jr., and Ariel

From left to right: John Wulu Jr., Mommy Wulu and John's wife, Josephine

My daughter, Elizabeth and her family: Elizabeth and youngest daughter, Nakeya (back); oldest daughter Dominica, her husband, Steve and son Diandre', son, Nathan not on picture

My grandson, Francois Wulu
Dominique Jr

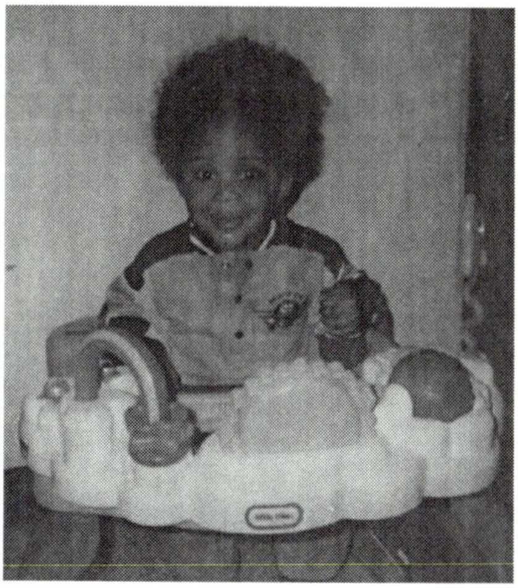

Baby John McKay, my grandson named after
me

My grand children

My three sons: left to right - Aaron, John Jr.,
Francois-Caesar

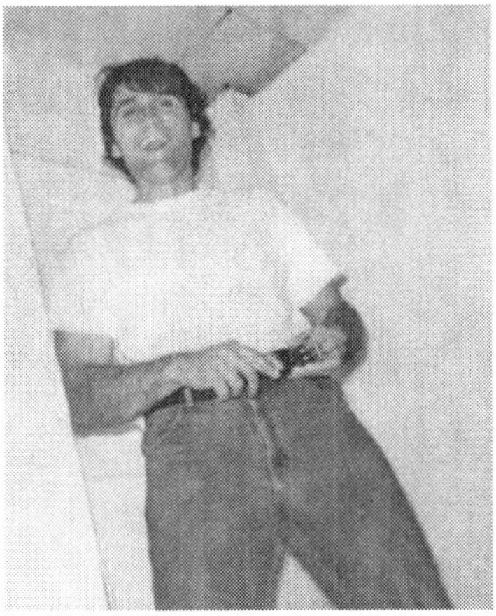

My daughter, Ruth's husband, Halit

Me and Mommy and our
grandchildren at our Day Care

Mommy and her Day care Children

Me and Mommy and our daughter Kaller

I am in the wedding party of our daughter, Comfort Doeley

Mommy Wulu is beautifully posing

Chapter 5
Gods' blessings;
My bride, My Family

On August 26, 1957, I was employed by the Monrovia Port Management Company at the Freeport of Monrovia, Liberia. I was very pleased and happy when I got the job. After work that day, I went home and told my beautiful young girl how the Port Management Company employed me as a permanent employee. She was very glad and happy. Both of us thanked the Lord for the job.

By September and October of that year, it was clear to me that my job was permanent. I informed my beauty that I wanted to get married to her that year, in December 1957. I said to her, "You know I love you and I believe you love me too. I want to tell my missionaries about our marriage at the earliest part of December 1957."

"It is no problem with me," she said. "You know very well that I love you very deeply in my heart. I would inform my guardians if you really want us to get married in December of this year."

I said, "Yes this year, in December." I said in my heart, 'I love the fine girl and she loves me also. Why shouldn't we get married in December?' We would pray together and ask God to make it possible, because this was a good plan. We prayed about it. I informed my missionaries and she told her guardians about our plan to get married in December.

John Nimley Wulu, Sr., AA, BA

As both of us were anxious to get married, a wedding dress was purchased in November. I also had my suit ready for the wedding. We informed Rev. John Hurston, the missionary I was living with, who agreed to perform the marriage ceremony, and we told Mr. Lawrence Gboeway, who was to give his cousin away to me. We also informed my loved one's cousin, Edmond Newton, and my mission mate Joe Tarty, and many others about our wedding.

On December 4, 1957, Rev. Hurston joined my beautiful and loved girlfriend, Miss Minnie Kyne, and me, John Nimely Wulu, a handsome young fellow, in holy matrimony, and we became husband and wife. God blessed our marriage. It was a very happy wedding, because we had completed our desires.

We were grateful to the Lord God, who made it possible for us to be pronounced husband and wife by Rev. Hurston. Both of us expressed our sincere thanks and appreciation to all who through the help of God made our marriage possible. As a husband, I expressed my special thanks and appreciation to Mr. Lawrence Gboeway, who happily gave his cousin, Miss Minnie Kyne, to me, who became Mrs. Minnie Kyne Wulu. I also gave a big thanks to the missionaries who raised me and assisted me greatly in learning about God the Father through the gospel message of Jesus Christ.

After our little wedding, my beautiful wife Minnie Wulu and I went home and had a good and enjoyable night. On Sunday morning we dressed beautifully and went to our Assembly of God church. My missionaries were very pleased to see us there. We were happy that we attended church service. We went home, and my beautiful wife prepared a lovely and delicious dinner which we enjoyed.

The following morning, my dear wife prepared a nice breakfast for me. After eating, I kissed her and went to work. With happiness in my heart when I arrived at work, I informed my co-workers that I had gotten married and had a beautiful wife. They congratulated me and wished me a blessed marriage and a successful life.

60

The Miracles and Riches of God

After work, I went straight home. My pretty wife was preparing our dinner when she saw me, came over, and kissed me. She said, "How was work today"?

I replied, "Everything was okay at my workplace." I went in the room and rested for two good hours, then she came in and said, "Honey boy, the food is ready." I got up and went in the bathroom, washed my mouth, and went to sit at the table. She came and joined me. The food was very delicious.

It was very obvious that we loved one another, and God had blessed us because He had given us our first beautiful child. Both of us were very happy when we had our first pretty child, named Ruth. Our union had been blessed with a kid, so there was great happiness in our home. We had a young child to play with.

One day while my fat-legged and long-haired wife and I were relaxing and playing with one another, I said, "I used to be very attracted to females, as you attracted me. Now I want to maintain a good character and have a religious life pleasing to God. I also want to be admired by my missionaries as a faithful and good young fellow who aims at a better future with honesty."

For my good character and religious ways, along with the admiration of my missionaries for my faithfulness, they gave me a Sunday School teacher position. And because I was committed and did a good job, I was promoted to the Sunday School superintendent in our Assembly of God church. "Sweetheart," I said, "it seems like God is going to bless us with children. When I was in high school, I had a child by Miss Agnes, who lived near the new Assembly of God mission in Brewerville. The name of my beautiful child is Elizabeth. When I had the child, some of my classmates told me I would not continue my schooling. But God is good. Through God's great mercy and blessing, I went through high school. This means we have two children.

"Honey," I said to my wife, "now that I have a permanent job and we have land to build on, it would be good for us to build a house on

61

John Nimley Wulu, Sr., AA, BA

our land so that we and our children can live in our own house. At the end of March this year, 1958, I would like to start buying building materials to start building our house in Warwen near Jallah Town and Bassa Community. It will not be good for us to pay rent to people all the days of our lives."

"Yes, my dear," said my beauty, "I think it would be nice for us to build our own house. I would be happy for us to have our two children in our own home. This way, no one can trouble them."

So by the blessing power of the Lord, after March ended, I started buying building materials: cement, rocks, sand planks, sticks, nails, and zinc within the period of five months. Because of my anxiety, I started building the foundation of the house myself. Then my wife and I hired masons and carpenters, and they started the construction of our first house in Warwen.

The house had zinc roof, five bedrooms, one living room, one kitchen, and a small dining room. The walls were made of sticks and bamboo, which we daubed with mud. When the mud on the walls was dried, we plastered the wall with rich cement. Strong cement was applied to the floor, giving it a concrete finish, which then was covered with tiles. Ceiling boards were put overhead. The house had wooden doors and windows. It was painted white on the outside, and the doors and windows were painted brown.

Through the help of our Lord God, we moved into our new house on the 29th of February 1959. We were very happy. Being a young couple and anxious to move in our new home, we moved in before the house was completed. The house did not yet have the wooden doors, windows, concrete floor, and overhead ceiling boards, and the walls were not plastered. But we were happy to be in our own home. We completed our house while living in it.

After our marriage on December 4, 1957, it took us one year and three months to move into our own new house. We were more than happy in our home because we were not obligated to anyone for rent

62

The Miracles and Riches of God

payment—which meant we would never have to pay rent as long as we lived in Monrovia, Liberia.

We were grateful to God for our new home.

On March 4, 1960, our miraculous God blessed us with a boy child. We named him Emmanuel, which means God is with us. Our happiness was so great, and we were very grateful to God for the young child. This meant we had three children to take care of in our new home. We did not consider caring for three children a problem at all. The Divine Power had given us the energy and strength to raise our young ones. Because I had a job, I was very pleased that we were in the position to take care of our children.

From my personal opinion and observation, no one knows what the future holds for him. Only the Lord God of mercy knows the future for each individual. The best thing to do is to look up to the Creator, the God in whom we believe for our daily needs. God is our helper and provider.

My wife and I were young believers in the Lord. God gave us our first son. So we thought it wise to name him Emmanuel, meaning God is with us or God is in our midst. At the time, people came up to me and asked whether I had named my first son after myself, John Wulu Jr. I told them, "God comes first." God knows what is best. One year and a few days after our first son was born, the Almighty gave us a second son, whom we named John Wulu Jr. He was born on April 15, 1961. We now had four children to care for in our own home. For any person who puts God first and trusts Him, He will give that person the desires of his heart. My wife and I put God first, so he gave us our desire.

In the light of our happiness, my wife and I asked the Lord to give us strength and understanding of how to raise our children so they could grow in the right way of God.

It is a matter of fact that when a married couple puts their trust in the Lord and does the right thing, God multiplies their desirable riches. A year and three months and twenty-two days after John Jr. was

John Nimley Wulu, Sr., AA, BA

born, our blessed Creator gave us our third son. We named him Caesar Domu Wulu. We were very happy when our son was born. We praised God for multiplying our riches. While we were rejoicing over the birth of our son, I told my wife that the children were our riches. We must be very grateful to the Lord. Caesar Domu Wulu (now Francois Wulu Demonique) was born on August 7, 1962.

As the number of children increased, I told my wife that we must get a lady to help her with the children. When I was at work, she could not take care of the children by herself. She agreed with me. So we hired a lady by the name of Mary, commonly known as Gby-win. She was from the Grebo tribe in Maryland County.

It was a joy to care for our children. We had great admiration for them. We made it our duty to take them to church as they were growing up so God could bless them, guide them, and keep them healthy.

In this world, whatever we do, the Lord is watching us on how we show love to his precious gifts (the children) that He has given us. My wife Minnie and I have great love for our precious children. So after two years, four months, and twenty-three days, our Creator blessed us with our fourth son. We named him Solomon Wulu. Solomon was born on the 29th of December 1964 at Firestone Hospital, Harbel, Montserrodo County, Liberia.

My lovely wife Minnie Wulu and I were thankful and grateful to our Lord God for keeping His eyes upon us and multiplying our riches and for keeping us happy with our offspring.

When my wife was pregnant, the Lord put in my mind to think of how our five children would get education while the sixth one was on the way. So I talked to my wife about getting someone to teach our children in our house. She agreed for us to get a home tutor. This was in the earliest part of January 1964. I hired a young fellow by the name Avan Kofa to teach our children in our house. I turned my 12 by 8 feet bedroom into a classroom for the purpose of educating our children. I put a blackboard, a few chairs, and one or two tables in the room for the

64

The Miracles and Riches of God

teacher and children to use. While Mr. Kofa, a university student, was teaching our children in our home, our neighbors around us asked my permission to bring their children to my home to attend classes with my children. I know that the best thing to give a child is an education.

After about three months of teaching the children in my house, the number of students increased to more than ten. The 12 by 8 room became too small to hold the increasing number of children. It was obvious that God was blessing my wife and me with children and knowing that the best gift to give our children was education; I called my wife's attention to what the Lord was putting on my heart.

I said to her, "God has blessed us with children and even now you are pregnant with a young child. The classroom in our house cannot hold any more students. The Lord gives us more land. I want to establish a school for the purpose of giving our children and our neighbors' children an education! The children would be better off when they are educated."

In her response, she said, "Yes, it is a good thing to establish a school here in Warwen on our own land." I told her that I would build a school on our land in front of our house because I did not want the school building to be far from where we lived. Both of us agreed to establish a school and build it on our own land in Monrovia.

After praying about putting up a school building, I started buying building materials: blocks, cement, planks, rocks, and zinc for our school project. We hired masons and they started the construction work in April 1964. At the beginning, it was a two-room school building. After the masons laid the bricks to roof level, we hired carpenters who put a zinc roof over our two-room schoolhouse. Wooden doors and windows were put on. The masons laid a strong concrete cement floor and plastered the walls with good, rich cement. We painted the school building white and the doors and windows blue.

We thanked God that the school project was complete. We were very, very happy and pleased with our little school in the Warwen

John Nimley Wulu, Sr., AA,BA

Community that provided education to the children. We named the school John N. Wulu Elementary School, in honor of me.

While we were experiencing the happiness of putting up our little school building, I went to the Department of Education to apply for a school operation permit. The permit was granted to me after the building was inspected. My wife and I were very, very pleased and thankful to God, who made a way for us to establish a school.

I am with my son Emmanuel and his friend

I am with my son Emmanuel and his friends

LEFT: Mommy and I in our beautiful home in America.

BELOW: I posed for a picture after my family and I attended church services.

Mommy and I posed with our children: left to right - Solomon, Mommy, Francois, John Jr., Elizabeth, and myself.

Our daughter, Johnnette; Mommy and me (center); and family.

My wife, Mommy Wulu, on my right and her cousin, Arita on my left in London, 11/11/04

My wife and I at a family gathering

We are celebrating at my son John Jr.'s home. We posed for a family picture

RIGHT: I gave Comfort Doeley away to her husband in Boston

BELOW: Our niece Agnes Wah, me and Mommy

Mommy and I posed with our son, Francois, and his family: Bottom left to right: Wife, Orla; Mommy and Papa; son, Francois. Their children (back) left to right: Dominique, Pierre, Ashley, Francois Jr. and Famatta (front center)

Mommy and I posed with son, John Jr. and his family: Jackie and Prince John (back); front left to right: Wife, Josephine; Mommy, Jaleel, me and son, John Jr., son, Jermane not on picture.

Mommy and I with our grandchildren and Stephanie holding our grand daughter.

CHAPTER 6
BUILDING AND ESTABLISHING MY FIRST SCHOOL

John N. Wulu Elementary School was opened in the second week in February 1965 in Warwen, Monrovia, Liberia. We started the school with twenty-five students and one female teacher, named Mrs. Lucy Subah. She was a good teacher. During the first semester, as the students increased in number, I employed one additional teacher, by the name of Mary William. Our neighbors were happy that we had opened a school in our community. Now their children would have an opportunity to attend the school in the Warwen Community. They could walk to the school and not have to pay for transportation. Parents could walk with their kindergarten children to John Wulu Elementary School, situated right in the center of the community.

Many parents expressed their thanks and appreciation to my wife, Mrs. Minnie Wulu, and me for such an idea of building a school. I told them that they should thank the Lord that made a way for us to put up the building for our children and their children to have a place to attend school and obtain education. I told the parents that the best gift they could give their children was education. When the kids obtain educational knowledge in school, they will be better off in the future. It is obvious that a better future is for those who prepare themselves for it.

John Nimley Wulu, Sr., AA,BA

At the end of John Wulu Elementary School's first year in operation, the

enrollment was ninety-five students in the morning section. In Liberia the Department of Education made provision so that children who are not privileged to attend school in the morning could attend school in the afternoon.

As we were progressing in the field of education, our blessing God of the eternal world gave us our third beautiful baby girl, who was born on December 7, 1966, with lots of hair. We named her Minnie Wulu after her mother. She came one year, eleven months, and eight days after the birth of Solomon Wulu. We thanked the Lord for giving us precious children.

In the second year of our little new school, we opened two sections, the morning and afternoon sections. We had two teachers in the morning section and two teachers in the afternoon section. In the second year of school operation, the enrollment of students increased to two hundred. One hundred students attended the morning section and one hundred students attended the afternoon section.

I was one of those who had fallen into the afternoon school section in 1949 at J. B. McCrithy Afternoon School in Monrovia, Liberia. When I was young in the fifth grade, Rev. Jensen and his wife took me from Tchien Mission, Eastern Province, now Grand Gedeh County, to Monrovia to live with other missionaries and attend school. I was very pleased and grateful to the Almighty that I was privileged to be in school.

From my personal observation, the Department of Education in Liberia did a good thing when they authorized the operation of afternoon schools, mostly for servant children. The majority of students who attended school in the afternoon were the servants of the upper class in Liberia. And most of the servants were the children of the Liberian uneducated natives who lived in the interior parts of Liberia.

The Miracles and Riches of God

The process went somewhat like this. Because the majority of the natives were uncivilized and uneducated and wanted their children to have a better life than they'd had, a native parent would give his or her son or daughter to a so-called civilized educated couple to raise and provide education for the child. In return, the child would become a servant to that so-called educated civilized couple and their children. The children of these civilized couple (guardians) would attend school in the morning while the majority of the servant children stayed home and did housework. They would clean up, wash and iron clothes, cook food for their guardians and their children, and take care of the yard. And in the afternoon, when the children of the guardians returned home from school to their clean house, then the servant children would get ready and go to afternoon school.

When I first came to Monrovia, I fell in the afternoon students category. After looking at my background, I praise God, who gave me a good thinking faculty to establish a learning institution for the servants to get an education. Because we had a good intention for the young ones to obtain knowledge for a better life, my wife Mrs. Minnie Wulu and I were privileged to be the proprietors and founders of John Wulu Elementary School.

I was the first principal of John Wulu Elementary School, and my wife Mrs. Minnie Wulu was the first vice principal of John Wulu Elementary School in Monrovia, Liberia, West Africa.

I give God the glory. After working seven good years at the Monrovia Port Management Company at the Freeport of Monrovia, Liberia, my wife and I established our own business, the school. It was just a matter of strong determination and ambition of a wife and husband working cooperatively with a firm desire to be successful in life. And through the power of the Creator, we founded our little school.

I held two jobs after the opening of my own school. I served as principal in my school and worked at the Monrovia Port Management Company at the Freeport of Monrovia. It really pays to create your

73

John Nimley Wulu, Sr., AA, BA

own business. I created a second job for myself and other people too. I employed teachers in my school, and they in turn imparted their knowledge to the young children in the school.

When I observed that our little two-room schoolhouse was overcrowded, my wife and I decided to add two additional rooms to the school building. I purchased concrete blocks, bags of cement, sand, planks, nails, sticks, ceiling boards, gallons of paint, and rocks.

We hired masons and they laid two rooms rock foundation attached to the school building. They completed the walls up to roof level using concrete blocks. We then called in carpenters, who put up the roof over the two-room addition, using planks, nails, and zinc. The carpenters made doors and windows for the two-room addition and put them on also.

I called the masons back to put the concrete floor in and plaster the walls inside and outside, which they did very nicely. To make the school building look beautiful, I hired painters and they painted the walls white on the outside and blue on the inside. They even painted the doors and windows blue.

The school building was very attractive and beautiful. While we were admiring our beautiful school building, the God of Christ Jesus put us in the mood of happiness and admiration by giving us our fifth son on the 14th of January 1968. We named him Alexander Molar Wulu. We praised God for His many blessings upon us.

At the end of our little school's third year of operation, in February 1968, the additional two rooms were ready to be used for classes. We were pleased. Now we could take in additional students and at the same time reduce the overcrowded classes to forty-five students per teacher. This also meant that we could enroll one hundred eighty students in the morning section and one hundred eighty students in the afternoon section in our four-room schoolhouse, in accordance with the education law in Liberia, which calls for forty-five students per class.

The Miracles and Riches of God

Being so anxious, in the third week in February 1968, we started registering students. We registered one hundred sixty new students, in addition to the two hundred students from the previous year. Increasing the number of students in my school enabled me to employ four new teachers. Through the blessed hand of God, this put me in the book of employers.

I want to emphasize our main purpose of founding the school. Our main objective of establishing a school was to give our children an education. We also wanted to extend that opportunity to our neighbors' children as well as to children who did not live in our neighborhood.

We wanted to encourage and advise parents to bring their children to our school to get an education or send their children to any other school to obtain an education because education is one of the essential gifts to give to a child.

The second purpose of establishing a school was to create jobs for those who were not employed and were in need of jobs; to recruit people who had teaching skills and were willing to impart their skills or knowledge to young children as well as old people who wanted to gain knowledge or wanted to learn. It is very obvious that when people are educated, they render good services to their people and their country.

My wife and I had our interest in the field of education. I served as a teacher at the Assembly of God mission school. My wife, Mrs. Minnie Wulu, was employed as a kindergarten school teacher by Mrs. Ora Hourton at the Bassa Community School, founded by Rev. and Mrs. Hourton in Monrovia, Liberia.

She got the teaching job at Ora Hourton Kindergarten School when our first son Emmanuel Wulu was crawling. She started teaching her kindergarten class under the breadfruit tree on the campus, and later on her class was moved to the porch of the kindergarten school building. All of the kindergarten classrooms in the school building were full; therefore, my wife had to teach her students on the porch.

75

John Nimley Wulu, Sr., AA,BA

I made the first blackboard that she used to teach the students under the breadfruit tree and on the porch of the Ora Hourton Kindergarten School building. I also made the stand on which she placed the blackboard. The blackboard was placed in an upright position. I made the blackboard and the stand because I was happy that my wife got a teaching job. It is a matter of fact that a teacher must have a blackboard to illustrate her work as she teaches, writing down the numbers and alphabets for the children to see, practice, and learn.

My wife's starting salary was between $20 and $25 per month. We were satisfied with the salary because we were young people just coming up. Food was not costly. A hundred-pound bag of rice cost $5. A pound of beef cost less than a dollar. Deer, monkey, and even elephant meat was very cheap. Fish of all kinds were not expensive. Grains were also very cheap.

Mrs. Ora Hourton paid my wife privately. But later, she was placed on the government payroll by the Department of Education, and her salary was raised to $35 per month. She was then transferred to the Government Kindergarten School at the Fredrick Building on Camp Johnson Road away from Ora Hourton Kindergarten School.

In the interest and safety of our children, I humbly and honestly asked the Department of Education to transfer teacher Minnie Wulu, my dear wife, from the Government Kindergarten School to my private school, John Wulu Elementary School, in Warwen near Bassa Community, in Monrovia, Liberia.

As we requested, my wife was transferred to our private school as a subsidized teacher. Both of us were enthusiastically happy about the transfer because she would work in our school, be close to our children, and could keep her eye on them. This move also gave her the opportunity to render her service full time in the morning and afternoon sections at the school. Very importantly, with my wife working as the vice principal at the school, she could keep her eye on the students and teachers.

The Miracles and Riches of God

My wife was very pleased because she no longer had to travel a long distance to her job. Her workplace was now right in front of her house, about a minute or two away. She could see her house through her office window. It was just to my taste that my wife was now working in our little school and she could keep her eye on our children and the students in our school.

In the midst of our happiness concerning the transference of my lovely wife, Teacher Wulu, the Lord added to our happiness by giving us our fourth beautiful baby girl on the first of May 1969. We named her Johnnette P. Wulu. We thanked God for giving us more riches. Our children are the precious riches from the Lord. They are worth more to us than material riches, silver, or gold.

It is always a good thing to remember people who brought you up and helped you through life. So as the Lord began to increase my blessings, I began to think about the missionaries who raised me and taught me about the Lord Jesus that made me become a Christian.

The missionaries that imparted my life with Christian knowledge were mostly from the United States, with the exception of Rev. I. T. Jensen and his wife, the first missionary couple that taught me Christian doctrine. They were from Denmark. They were the missionaries who took me in at their Tchien mission, in Zwedru, Tchien District, now Grand Gedeh County, to live there and attend school.

At Tchien Mission, I learned to read and write and also learned about the Lord Jesus Christ. Miss LePeirce was my first beginners class teacher. She came from America. Then there were Rev. John Hurston and his wife, who took me to live at their mission house in Monrovia, when the Jensens were going to Denmark on vacation.

Miss Mary Martin, Miss Anna Staford, known as Miss Anna S. Richard, and Miss Florine Bassey were all missionaries from America. They all assisted me greatly in getting my education. I am very thankful to all of them.

I gave my cousin, Sophia Doeley, away to her husband

Papa and Mommy with Ruth and her husband, Halit and children;
Lakesha holding her daughter and Howard

My family gathered at my son John Jr.'s house

Papa and Mommy in the middle posing with six of their ten children. Left to right Elizabeth, John Jr., Papa, Mommy, Aaron, Kaller, Francois, Ruth

My son Francois-Caesar

My son Demonique and wife Thabo when they got married.

Mommy and I are with our son Demonique WuluWilson, his wife Thabo holding our new born grandson, Demonique Jr

My birthday celebration at my daughter Kaller and her husband, Joseph McKay's home seeing embracing. Left from back to front, Valerie, Timothy, Famatta, Mommy, Francois Jr., Papa holding baby John, Jaleel, John Jr., Jackie, Prince John, Joseph Jr.

From left to right - Papa Wulu, my granddaughter, Lakesha, my wife, Minnie Wulu, and my daughter, Elizabeth

John Wulu Jr. and family. Left to right - John Jr., Jaleel, Prince John and Jackie displaying their academic awards, and wife Josephine

My son Emmanuel's daughter Kara

My son Emmanuel's daughter Valerie

CHAPTER 7

During this time in my life, as I was experiencing the Lord's increased blessings upon my life, I began to think about the country the missionaries came from who turned my life in the right direction. Through the newspaper, I started reading about the United States. I began to follow the general elections of the United States by watching the political debates on television. Because of my interest and liking for the American people, I began to read the history of this great nation. The United States got her independence in 1776. General George Washington was the first President of United States, 1789–1797; John Adams was the second President of United States, 1797–1801; . . . James Monroe was the fifth President of United States, after whom the capital city Monrovia of Liberia was named.

On television, I saw former President Richard M. Nixon run against the late John F. Kennedy for the presidency, but Nixon was defeated. Four years later, Nixon ran against Lyndon B. Johnson, Nixon was defeated. He later went to his own state, California, and tried for the governor's office, but he was not successful. Nixon did not give up. In 1968 he ran again for the office of the President. This time he won the presidential election and became thirty-seventh President of the United States.

I admire former President Richard M. Nixon for his courage. In view of Richard M. Nixon's determination, persistence, and courage,

John Nimley Wulu, Sr., AA,BA

I wrote him a letter. In my letter I stated, "Mr. President, to you defeat means success. You were defeated two times for the office of the President, you did not allow that to deter or discourage you. You ran again, and this time you won the presidential election and now you are the President of United States of America. My entire family and I have strong admiration for you. I have my own school in my name, John N. Wulu Elementary and Junior High School. But I decided to rename my school in your honor and call it Richard M. Nixon Institute. The school is located in Monrovia, the capital city of Liberia, West Africa.

President Nixon replied to my letter through the American Embassy in Monrovia, Liberia, and said it was okay for me to name my school in his honor. But he had no financial support to give the institute. My family and I were very pleased that we got an "okay" response from Nixon to name the school after him. In 1970, we named the school Richard M. Nixon Institute.

As a man who aims high with strong determination, while still working at the Port Management Company, I started taking courses at the University of Liberia. Through persistent effort, I received my associate of arts (AA) degree in accounting from the University of Liberia, December 1971.

On the 21st of April 1972, the Lord blessed us with our sixth boy child. We named him Aaron Benima Wulu. Benima means "let it be so; John, you and your wife Minnie have plenty children, so let it be so now." We were very, very grateful to the Lord for an additional son.

During that time, our four-room school building had gotten overcrowded. With my desire to give more young and old people an education, I started a building project for expansion. I purchased bags of cement, blocks, rocks, sand, sticks, zinc, nails, gallons of paint, and ceiling boards to build an eight-room school building on our land in Warwen on Capital By-Pass, near the University of Liberia in Monrovia.

The Miracles and Riches of God

In Liberia, most home owners purchase building materials and then call masons and carpenters to put up the house or buildings. So after purchasing the building materials for our second school building, we hired masons. They started the construction work on my project. After they laid the rock foundation and the block walls up to roof level, we hired carpenters, who built the roof over our eight-room schoolhouse.

When the second school building project was completed, we thanked God. We were very, very happy and pleased with our second school building in the Warwen community to provide education to the young children and older people who wanted to get education.

We taught the Bible in our school, because we believe that biblical education is very important.

In my personal opinion, learning has no end as long as the Lord gives me life and strength. So with more ambition and as the chief head and founder of learning institutions, I did more studies at the University of Liberia. On the 10th of December 1974, I obtained a bachelor of arts degree in business administration and management. I was very happy that I got a four-year B.A. college degree.

The eight-room school building is located opposite the capitol building and near the University of Liberia. At the beginning of 1972, I hired sixteen qualified teachers for the new school building—eight teachers in the morning section, and eight teachers in the afternoon section.

In the third week of February, we started registration. We registered two hundred twenty students in the morning section and two hundred twenty students in the afternoon section. We had one hundred fifty students in the night section. The total number of students enrolled in both school buildings was nine hundred fifty.

After renaming the school in honor of the former President Richard M. Nixon, the school was raised to high school level. Richard M. Nixon High School put out its first graduates in 1975. I was the principal from the founding date up to the institute's first high school graduation.

85

John Nimley Wulu, Sr., AA, BA

I give Almighty God the glory and praise for giving me young, good, and educated teachers who worked strongly with me and imparted their knowledge and skills to the young and older students at John Wulu Kindergarten, John Wulu Elementary and Junior High School, and Richard M. Nixon Institute in Monrovia, Liberia, West Africa.

Many, many thanks to all the people—teachers, registrars, matrons, and cooks—who worked and assisted me from the founding dates of the above-mentioned schools. I pray to the Lord to bless them and give them more knowledge, skills, and strength to continue to assist the young and old to get an education.

Thanks to all our children for assisting us with the establishment of our institution. Some of you have worked very hard in the school. So I am very thankful to all of you for your great assistance. If we did not have you, we would not have established the above-mentioned schools. Through the great power of the Lord, we were able to establish the schools.

Remember that God has brought you in this world through us with His blessing hand. You pray and thank Him every day.

While holding the principal position at the above-mentioned schools, I served as supervisor at one of the accounts sections and also served as the acting chief supervisor of the cashier department at the Monrovia Port Management Company. I was also authorized to deposit money for the Monrovia Port Management Company in the Bank of Monrovia, Liberia.

As I was working on my God-given permanent job, I married a beautiful girl, Minnie Kyne, daughter of Paramount Chief Domu Kyne Wilson of Pleebo, Maryland County, Liberia. We had children and built our first house. We founded our own private schools, constructed two concrete school buildings, and built our second concrete home for dwelling in Warwen, on the Capital By-Pass near the University of Liberia. I am telling you the story of how Divine God blessed us.

The Miracles and Riches of God

While my wife and I worked cooperatively, we purchased a plat of land on Bushrod Island, near St. Paul Bridge. This land already had two buildings on it. One of the buildings became John Wulu Elementary and Junior High School. This was the second school we founded. Thanks to God that the United Nations Development Program took down the old building and constructed a new one on the same spot for John Wulu Elementary and Junior High near St. Paul Bridge. We are very grateful to the UNDP.

After working for a solid eighteen years and six months at the Port Management Company at the Freeport of Monrovia, Liberia, I have seen the great power of God, how He blessed me and my wife in many, many ways; then I realized the greatness of the Lord God. I bowed before God and prayed, saying, "Thank you, Almighty God, for your loving kindness and the many blessings you have bestowed upon me. I honestly pray to count my blessings you have bestowed upon us. I honestly pray to count our blessings one by one and never to forget them."

The Lord has shown me the way and has given me strength to understand what I have done for a better tomorrow. Through God's goodness and assistance, I got a college education, which enabled me to head our schools.

I enthusiastically decided to join my lovely wife, Mrs. Minnie Kyne Wulu, who resembled her dear mother, Noon Kalor of Pleebo, Maryland County, Liberia, to guide and prepare our children for a better future.

In view of my great interest in my precious children, and in order for me to guide and prepare them for a brighter future, I resigned my position at the Monrovia Port Management Company in 1976 after eighteen years and six months of service.

I joined my beautiful wife in our school, Richard M. Nixon Institute, where I continued my principalship. Richard M. Nixon Institute was placed under the Monrovia Consolidated School System, and I became a government school principal. I was paid by the Liberian government.

John Nimley Wulu, Sr., AA,BA

It is a fact that whenever a person is not self-centered and does something good for the benefit of others and his country, God will surely reward him. That good deed or good intention will surely bring honor and reward to the person.

I was honored and awarded a certificate for establishing and erecting school buildings in Monrovia, Liberia. With the efforts of the superintendent of Monrovia Consolidated School System, Mr. John H. Manster, the Deputy Secretary of Education, the Honorable Mr. Duncan, presented certificates to all of us who founded schools and erected school buildings in Monrovia, Liberia, for our kind interest in education and our great contribution in the field of education to our country.

By the help of God, while I was working as the principal of Richard M. Nixon Institute, my wife and I purchased land in Zwedru, the capital city of Grand Gedeh County, and in Ziah Town, the Headquarters of Konobo District, and built a house with a zinc roof in our district.

My wife and I with our youngest son, Aaron and his family. Mommy & Papa (back); left to right - Aaron, his wife, Crystal, Avner, Aaron Jr., Arial, and Sir Christopher

Mommy and I with our son Aaron and his family. Top row left to right - Aaron, Mommy, myself, Crystal. Bottom row - Avner, Aaron Jr., Ariel, Sir-Christopher.

My son Francois-Caesar with his children. Left to right - Famatta, Francois Jr., Ashley, Pierre and Dominique in the back

*Four of my grand children. Left to right –
Christopher, Ariel, Benjamin, Joseph Jr.*

*My grand daughter,
Lakesha Bondurant.*

*Addy, my son, Solomon's
daughter.*

Three of my grand children. Left to right - Eddie, Valerie, Kara

My wife holding Demonique Wilson Jr., our grand son; his mother, Thabo in the center and me.

November 28, 2002 on my birthday, Mommy is laughing.

My wife, Minnie Wulu, my son, Demonique Wulu Wilson and me at his house

My wife and I in London

My son, Demonique and I on the train on our way to London, November 11, 2004

Chapter 8
God's Protection

When my people in Konobo District saw the good work I did in our district and in the capital city, Monrovia, they petitioned me to represent them and serve in the Senate.

Whenever I am faced with a decision, problem, or anything I want to do, I always first put it before the Lord. I remembered many years back as a laborer boy, I was told to go to Sinoe with other laborers to get petroleum for the radio station that was being built in Zwedru. As I was walking on Sinoe Road going back to Zwedru with petroleum, I wondered what to do about my life. Not knowing what to do, I prayed to God to show me the way to go, because I did not know where to go or what to do. The Lord in His grace and mercy showed me the way by directing me to Tchien Mission on March 18, 1945. The missionaries accepted me at their mission, where I learned to read and write and also learned about the Lord. God later made a way for me to go to Monrovia, the capital city.

In another instance, in 1951, I was in the eighth grade in Monrovia and saw a friend named Paul Thomas, the boy who Rev. Jensen asked to take me to the boys' house my first day at Tchien Mission. Paul was working in the Liberia police force. He asked me to join the police force. He said, "John, you are qualified with an eighth-grade education. Some of the people in the police force cannot read or write." This was 1951.

John Nimley Wulu, Sr., AA,BA

I put the police force request before the Lord. I said, "Lord, if it is good for me to be in the police force, permit me to join tomorrow, but if it is not good for me, let me be sick tomorrow." And the following day, I was very sick. So I did not join the police force.

So I put my district people's petition to serve them in the Liberian Senate before God. I prayed, saying, "Lord, please give me what will be good for me; do not give me what will not be good for me, even I do not care when my heart wants it."

So I ran for a senatorial position in Monrovia, Liberia, West Africa, in October 1979, but I did not get it. The Lord knew that the senatorial position was not good for me so, I did not get it.

Those who were elected in October 1979 were sworn into office in January 1980, but they stayed in office only in February and March, because on April 12, 1980, a coup took place. The late President William R. Tolbert was overthrown, and Sergeant Samuel Doe took control of Liberia as head of state. Some of the elected senators and other officials were thrown in jail.

It is very obvious that God knows what tomorrow will bring, but we do not know what tomorrow has for us. So I am grateful to the Lord for not permitting me to win the senatorial post. It is good to ask God to give you what is good for you.

When Samuel K. Doe took control of Liberia as head of state, a decree or order was issued that the Senate and House of Representatives were dissolved. Within the period of few weeks, a Redemption Council was founded, and Doe was elected as its chairman.

Some members of the Redemption Council took the places of senators and representatives. New superintendents were appointed by the head of state, Samuel K. Doe, in all the counties in Liberia under his control. After one year, two months, and fourteen days of the Samuel K. Doe administration, I was appointed executive director of the Unity Conference Center, on June 26, 1981, by the Doe government, through

The Miracles and Riches of God

the effort of Dr. Harry F. Nayou, Minister of Presidential Affairs at the Executive Mansion, Monrovia.

My wife Mrs. Minnie Wulu took over the principal position at Richard M. Nixon Institute.

The Unity Conference Center is part of the Executive Mansion. The employees of the Unity Conference Center are employees of the Executive Mansion. So I was one of the officials of the Executive Mansion. The Unity Conference Center was built by the Organization of Africa Unity (OAU), in Virginia, near the St. Paul River, during the administration of the late President William R. Tolbert. It was purposely built for international conferences and meetings held in Monrovia, Liberia, by the OAU.

When I was appointed as an executive director of the UCC, I served as chief administrator and supervised all works and activities held at the center. I had five supervisors plus eighty employees under my control at the Unity Conference Center. The supervisors were Harry Jorlon, Stephen Corber, Rachel Alison, Rachel Nayou, and Kamara. Sarah Tarley was an assistant supervisor.

The center had its own accounts department, headed by Mr. Harry Jorlon. He was the supervisor of the accounts department and my special assistant. I authorized Mr. Jorlon to supervise activities at the center during my absence on special occasions.

At the center's accounts department, we prepared our own budget and payroll and kept accounts records of all money collected from conferences and meetings. Monies collected were deposited in the Unity Conference Center account in the bank. This money was used to cover expenses at the Unity Conference Center. But the amount collected from conferences and meetings in a year was not enough to maintain the center. So we prepared a yearly government budget in writing, listing item by item the amount needed to maintain the Unity Conference Center in a year.

John Nimley Wulu, Sr., AA,BA

We had a security section at the Unity Conference Center. The security section was headed by Chief of Security Isaac Doe. There were seven security personnel guarding the center. There was also a cafeteria section, headed by Miss Mary Geko. Miss Mary Geko had other ladies preparing food for the employees and other visitors for sale. This generated additional revenue for the conference center.

Although we were considered employees of the Executive Mansion, our workplace was at the Unity Conference Center. This location is about nine to ten miles away from the Executive Mansion. As the executive director of the UCC, I drove ten miles from my house to the UCC office. The Unity Conference Center had two large buses that picked up UCC employees for work and took them home in the evening.

As one of the top government officials, I was assigned a driver. I was also assigned a secretary, named Mark Richards, who did my typing. The UCC had two assistant secretaries, Musu Weght and Comfort Doeley, who did the typing for the UCC. The secretaries were paid by Liberia government.

The Unity Conference Center building is large department that had many conference rooms and offices. Located in the UCC was a presidential office that had a connecting sitting room, a secretarial room, and a presidential bar. The center had a very large conference room that held one thousand and more persons. The building was used for many purposes. It has very large ballroom and dining rooms. It has small bars for entertainment. It has interpreter rooms and many other rooms for useful purposes.

At the Unity Conference Center, the executive director controls some villas and small prefab houses at the OAU Village. The executive director controls and supervises all activities pertaining to the Unity Conference Center. Because the director has authority over the center, the head of state wrote him to provide three villas, typewriters, copy machines, and other equipment to Dr. Amos Sawyer, chairman of the

96

The Miracles and Riches of God

Constitution Commission, for the preparation of the new constitution in 1982.

Being that the UCC building was a large department with more facilities, when the general election was held in October 1985, the Election Commission asked me, the executive director of the UCC, to permit them to count the ballots; and I gave them permission to do so. The Honorable Hamet Harmon was then the chairman of the Election Commission.

The party of Samuel K. Doe, head of state, won the general presidential election in 1985, and his inauguration was held in January 1986. Samuel K. Doe was sworn into office as President of the Republic of Liberia. He was the first aboriginal, or native, Liberian to be President of Liberia.

I thank God and give Him praise for affording me the opportunity to obtain an education which enabled me to serve my government and country in various positions. It is very obvious that good education enables a person to obtain a good job or position. The last position I held in Monrovia, Liberia, was an executive director, earning $1,300.00 per month, my highest salary there. I worked nine years at the Unity Conference Center. I left the position because of civil war.

While I was on this job, the civil war started in Liberia on December 23, 1989, in Nimba County. Charles Taylor's rebels were killing people from county to county and city to city. Some of the people who ran away from Nimba County came to my house and informed me that my name was on the list of people Charles Taylor and his people were planning to kill. His rebel group had planned to kill me and my entire family.

Within three or four months, the news was all around that Charles Taylor and his rebels had planned to kill all government officials who were working with President Samuel K. Doe and that President Doe would be killed also.

John Nimley Wulu, Sr., AA,BA

It is a matter of fact that God is good. I thank the Lord God for giving me wisdom and understanding of what is good for my wife, children, grandchildren, and me.

I will praise God for making a way for me to send my children to the United States one by one between 1975 and 1988 through his blessing power before the civil war broke out in Liberia. Only two of our children were with us when rebels entered Monrovia and started killing people.

Then our children in the United States started calling us to leave Monrovia because the rebels were in the city killing people on the other side of Monrovia, and our son Francois Wulu Demonique continued calling us, saying, "Papa, you and Mammie and the other children must go to Ivory Coast or any country so the rebels cannot kill you."

Being that the children advised us to leave Monrovia so we would not be killed by the rebels, I immediately sent my wife, Mrs. Minnie Wulu, and our grandchildren to Sierra Leone on June 26, 1990, and I stayed behind in Monrovia with the intention to follow them later.

But on the following day, June 27, 1990, my daughter Elizabeth Wulu Brown called me from the United States and said, "Papa, where are you?" I answered and said I was there in Monrovia, Liberia. She said, "You must leave Monrovia!" And I said okay, and I put the phone down. Then within two or three minutes, she called again and said to me, "What did I say?" and I answered and said, "You said I must leave Monrovia." Then she said, "Do not blame us if you fail to leave Monrovia because the rebels are in Monrovia killing people according to the television news!"

Demonique, Mommy Wulu and me in London

My wife and I posing in front of Buckingham Palace in London

My wife and I standing near Buckingham Palace

My wife and I with her cousin, Arita Collins, standing near Buckingham Palace, London

My wife and I standing at the train station in London

My wife and I in London

Papa and Mommy Wulu standing in front of a monument near Buckingham Palace in London

We are at the church in London dedicating our newborn grandson. Holding the baby is my son Demonique and his wife Thabo. Next to them is my wife Minnie Wulu, myself and the church leaders.

I pledged to receive my U.S. citizenship.

I am about to sign my certificate of citizenship

My wife, Mrs. Wulu and son, Aaron pledged to receive their U.S. citizenship

I am signing my certificate of citizenship

I am receiving my certificate of citizenship

After receiving my certificate of citizenship.

My daughter, Johnnette is standing with me after receiving my certificate

CHAPTER 9
LIFE IN SIERRA LEONE

Because of the children's many urgings, I decided to leave Monrovia, Liberia. I asked my two children, Aaron and Alexander Wulu, to take me to Sierra Leone to my wife and grandchildren in a small town called Marlama on the Sierra Leone side near the Mano River. So Aaron and Alexander, who were with me in Monrovia, took me to Marlama, Sierra Leone, where my wife, Minnie Wulu, and grandchildren were.

We stayed in Marlama for two weeks, then I went back to Monrovia to view the condition in Liberia, but things were worse, so I asked Alexander and Aaron to take me back to Marlama. God is good. When I got there the following day, the Liberia and Sierra Leone border was closed because the civil war was getting worse in Liberia, and our two children could not come to us in Sierra Leone.

To make things complicated for us, the Sierra Leone soldiers took my new car from me at the Sierra Leone border in Marlama, so we faced difficulty in getting to Freetown, the capital city of Sierra Leone.

In order to let our children in the United States know that we were in Sierra Leone, I took a passenger car to Freetown, went to the telephone station, called the children in the United States, and informed them that my wife, grandchildren, and I were in Sierra Leone.

John T. Wulu Jr. answered the telephone and asked if we were all alive. I told him yes we all were living. He asked, "Where is mommy?"

103

I said that she was in Marlama, at the Sierra Leone border. He asked, "How much money do you need to bring mommy and the grandchildren to Freetown?" I told him to send whatever money he was able to. He told me that he would send $800 to us so that I could bring mommy and the grandchildren to Freetown from Marlama at the Sierra Leone border. He told me that I would get the money on the following Wednesday. I told him to send the money to Barclays Bank in Freetown, Sierra Leone.

On the Wednesday that John Wulu Jr. mentioned, I got the $800. So, on that same day I went to the telephone station, called John Wulu Jr., and said many thanks for the money you sent to us. I thank the Lord for opening a way for me always. While I was about to leave the telephone station, a Sierra Leone lady approached me and asked for my name. She in turn said that she was Yaelee Blarma, and asked if I was from Liberia. I said yes, and she continued, "Do you have your family with you here in Freetown?" I told her that my family was in Marlama at the border and that I was on my way to bring them.

Then she said, "You may bring your family to my house in Waterloo when you come along with them from Marlama." I expressed my thanks to her for her kind words and I agreed to look for her when I came to Freetown with my family.

So with happiness I went to my wife and grandchildren in Marlama. When I got to my wife, I told her about the $800 that John Wulu Jr. sent to us. I said, "I drew only three hundred dollars from Barclays Bank and left five hundred in, because I cannot travel with a lot of cash." She was very happy and praised God.

And I also informed my wife about Yaelee Blarma, whose heart the Lord God touched to invite my family to come and lodge in her house in Waterloo when we get to Freetown. Mommy was very pleased that God had provided a lodging place for us in Freetown.

We praised God that we had money to travel to Freetown. My wife, grandchildren, and I traveled to Freetown and went to the Liberian

The Miracles and Riches of God

Embassy, but the ambassador said that there was no room or sleeping place and I should have gotten an apartment before taking my family to Freetown.

We could not find Yaelee Blarma's house right away, so we went to the house of the parents of Deputy Minister of Finance Johnny Gaye's wife, Elizabeth, and stayed there for two or three days. After the third day, we found an apartment for US$100 per month. It was really a complicated problem for us.

But I went to the telephone station to inform our children in the United States that we were in Freetown, Sierra Leone. They all were pleased that we were alive and well there.

Our God is good. While getting out of the telephone station, I met Yaelee Blarma. She greeted me and said, "Are you and your family here now?" I told her yes. So I took her to my wife at the apartment we were renting; my wife, Minnie Wulu, was pleased when I introduced Mrs. Yaelee Blarma to her.

Mrs. Blarma told my wife that when she met me at the telephone station, she asked for the Wulu family to come and lodge in her house in Waterloo. "I thank God that you people are now in Freetown. I am ready to take the Wulu family to my house in Waterloo," she said.

Mrs. Wulu said to Mrs. Blarma, "Yes, it is true that my husband did tell me about your kind invitation to lodge in your house in Waterloo. I thank God for your kindness. We are ready to go along with you to your house."

With gladness, we took our luggage and went by passenger car to Mrs. Yaelee Blarma's house in Waterloo, where we lodged for seven months. Then later on we moved to a two-room apartment and stayed there for three months. When we left Monrovia, Liberia, we stayed at the border one month in Marlama on the Sierra Leone side. We stayed a good eleven months in Sierra Leone.

We are grateful to God for our children. It really pays to have children, because when our children found out that we were alive after

105

the war in Liberia and had gotten lodging, they began sending us money for food, rent, and transportation, after my new car had been taken from me by the Sierra Leone soldiers; and also to pay medical bills and other expenses. John T. Wulu Jr. sent $800, Kaller Minnie Wulu Mckay sent $400, and Elizabeth Wulu Brown sent $200. We left some of the money in Barclays Bank for Alexander and other grandchildren to use for food and rent payment.

We are very thankful to our children for the assistance they gave us when we were in Freetown, Sierra Leone, in 1990 and 1991.

My praise goes to God, who protected my wife and me on the dangerous hillside streets we traveled up and down to the Soldiers Barracks and Headquarters in Freetown. Through the help of the Lord, we got my car back.

So we were using the car from Waterloo to the center of Freetown to buy our foodstuffs every now and then. We were very comfortable having a car.

But in this world, people have different viewpoints. While we were in a happy mood because of Alexander and Aaron's safe return from the war and they were with us, my brother David came and took my car from my two children, Alexander and Aaron in Kinlima, near the Sierra Leone border.

He said the car belonged to him. But that was not true. The car was mine. I took the car to Sierra Leone. God knows the car was mine. But anyway, David did not have the car for long. The car crashed and did not last.

As a matter of fact, I love my brother David Q. Nimley (may his soul rest in peace). We are one mother's children and one blood through the blessed power of Divine God. We were very small when our dear mother, Karr-da Waylee, passed away and left us in this wonderful world. As an older brother, I stood by him and gave him advice.

But Almighty God did not forget about us. He made a way for me to go to Tchien Mission in Zwedru, Tchien District, Eastern Province,

The Miracles and Riches of God

now Grand Gedeh County. The Lord made a way, and David joined me at the mission. By the help of God, our good missionaries, Rev. and Mrs. Jensen, took me to Monrovia to attend school. Later on, my brother came and joined me in Monrovia.

While my brother was staying with me, he completed army training. The day he received his uniforms, he was promoted to corporal. And later on he was promoted to sergeant, because he was very active and good in his army platoon. Because of David's good performance in the army, he was sent to the United States for training. When he returned from the United States, he stayed at my house. Within a few years, he was promoted to various ranks in the Liberian Army: lieutenant, captain, major, colonel, and general. He did a very good job in the army.

Because I love my brother very dearly and wanted him to stay near me, I bought the land that he built his first house on in Warwen near Capital By-Pass in Monrovia, Liberia. I employed his wife, Esther Nimley, as a teacher, and him as a physical instructor in my school.

As we were in Freetown, we did not forget about our Lord. We prayed and He opened a way for us to get air tickets to travel to the United States. Kaller-Minnie Wulu Mckay sent $2,500 to us to pay for airline tickets to travel to the United States.

While we were trying to get the money from Barclays Bank in Freetown to purchase airline tickets, John T. Wulu Jr. sent two airline tickets for us to travel to the United States from Freetown, Sierra Leone. We were grateful to God and were very happy and pleased when we received the airline tickets.

The workers at Barclays Bank in Freetown did not treat us fairly, because they refused to give us United States dollars; instead, they gave us Sierra Leone paper money, which we could not use to pay for airline tickets.

When we took the Sierra Leone paper money to money changers, we received only $1,700. We lost US$800 because of Barclays Bank's

John Nimley Wulu, Sr., AA,BA

refusal to give us U.S. dollars. We would not have been cheated if Barclays Bank had given us U.S. dollars.

Out of the $1,700 (part of the money Kallar sent us for our ticket), Aaron Wulu used $1,500 to purchase his airline ticket in Freetown, Sierra Leone, to travel to the United States. He paid back the $1,500 to Kaller-Minnie Wulu Mckay. And my wife and I came on the airline tickets that John T. Wulu Jr. sent to us to come to the U.S. It pays to have good children, and I pray to God to pay them back double.

We thank God for the great and kind assistance of our children. We are still very grateful to all the children for the money and tickets they sent to us to come to the United States of America.

Family picture after receiving my certificate of citizenship

Family picture after I received my certificate. Back row – Francois-Caesar, Darlington, Kaller, Musa, Johnnette, Aaron; Front row - Mommy, myself, Elizabeth

The day I received my US citizenship.

Capt. Anna Cooper, my cousin

My cousin, Fineboy and me

Left to right: My wife and I , my cousin, Fineboy and his wife

I'm standing in front of a two room mat house. Former classrooms, which were torn down to, construct a new eight-room school building.

Mommy prepares dinner for mission team while daughter Elizabeth presents Papa with a father's day gift. A gift which elicits a big "WOW"from Papa

Left to right: Henry Nyanou, Mr. & Mrs. Fineboy and myself

LEFT: Papa, Mommy Wulu and daughter, Elizabeth when she visited us in Liberia.

BELOW: Left to right - Socelia Collins, Taryoner, Klowoo

CHAPTER 10
THE BLESSINGS OF GOD - NEW LIFE IN AMERICA

With happiness, on May 30, 1991, Thursday evening, we left Freetown, Sierra Leone, by KLM Airlines and arrived in Guinea within less than an hour; and we left Guinea after an hour and arrived at Amsterdam Airport in the morning on Friday. We changed airlines and left on that same Friday for Chicago, U.S. We arrived in Chicago at 4:00 p.m.

We left Chicago, Illinois, and went to John T. Wulu Jr. in Detroit, Michigan. We got there around 6:00 p.m. the same Friday, May 31, 1991. We were very thankful to the Lord, who brought us safely to the United States. John Wulu Jr., who came to pick us up from the airport, was very pleased to see us, and we were thankful to him for the $800 and the two airline tickets he sent to us in Freetown, Sierra Leone.

He quickly took us to his house in Detroit. His pretty wife, Josephine Wulu, was glad to see us and immediately prepared a delicious supper for us that evening, which we enjoyed. The following day, François Wulu Demonique who was very happy to see us, took me to the supermarket and purchased foodstuffs for us, which we consumed at John T. Wulu's home with gladness.

John Nimley Wulu, Sr., AA,BA

All the children were very pleased when they saw us and praised God, who saved us from the civil war. It was because of the civil war that we left Liberia and came to the United States of America for safety.

With anxiety to see the other children, who were living in Cleveland, Ohio, after staying at the home of John T. Wulu Jr. for one month (June) and some days, we left Detroit, Michigan, in July 1991 and went to Cleveland, Ohio, to see Elizabeth Wulu Brown, Kaller-Minnie Wulu Mckay, and Solomon Wulu.

In a happy mood, our children in Cleveland received us gladly. We were pleased to see them. We expressed our special thanks for their kind help to us when we were in Freetown, Sierra Leone.

While we were in Cleveland, Elizabeth, with the cooperation of her sisters and brother, filed my permanent residential document in August of 1991. I was very pleased that my residential documents were filed.

We stayed with Elizabeth until the later part of August 1991 and then we returned to Detroit, Michigan. And since John T. Wulu Jr. and his wife were not expecting us back in Detroit soon, our son Francois Wulu Demonique took us to the house of his American friend, Miss Stephanie. It really pays to have plenty of children. I thank God, who gave us plenty good, good, children.

We stayed at Stephanie's home more than one month. She was very kind and good to us. She gave us summer and winter clothes in Detroit. She was doing everything for our upkeep. We are grateful to the Lord for her great assistance. I remember she bought a fine white shirt for me.

Later, in October, we moved to John T. Wulu Jr.'s house in Detroit. We thank God that everything worked out fine in our interest. We found a two-room apartment on Wisconsin Avenue, where we moved at the end of October the same year.

My wife and I did not want to be a liability to my son and his wife. And also we were not interested in occupying their guest room for long time. So we moved to our apartment on Wisconsin Avenue. We lived on Wisconsin Avenue for one year.

The Lord is good. As I was praying hard to the Lord for my permanent residential card, the Department of Immigration sent for me in November 1991 for an interview. I passed the interview concerning my permanent resident document filed in August 1991. In December 1991, my residential card was mailed to me. I praised God and was very happy.

At Wisconsin, we were not lonesome. Our grandchildren, Musa Wulu, Lakisha Bondunrant, and Howard Bondurant, were living with us. Everything was fine with us.

At the latter part of 1992, our son Francois Wulu Demonique asked us to move into his house on Outer Drive in Detroit, on which he paid $5,000 as down payment to the owner. We moved there with gladness.

The Lord is good; he gave me good thinking faculty which enables me to think of the right things that would benefit me, my wife, and other people. So while we were on 8711 Outer Drive, Detroit, Michigan, I told my wife, Minnie Wulu, "I am always telling people that when they don't use their heads, their bodies suffer, and that they must hang their hats where their hands can reach. We are blessed to have a big house to ourselves, we must use our heads by doing Day Care in Detroit, then our bodies will not suffer." I said to her, "We will earn money when we are taking care of working mothers' children. We must do what we are able to do, because we have skill in child management. We are old teachers. You know we used our heads when we founded our own private schools in Liberia, West Africa."

While in the said house, we were privileged to attend Day Care Training. My wife, Mrs. Minnie Wulu, received a certificate, and we opened Minnie Wulu Day Care in Detroit, Michigan. We worked there as day care providers.

John Nimley Wulu, Sr., AA,BA

My wife and I have been blessed with God's precious gifts (children). So it appears that the Lord is doing the same with our offspring. In October 1994, our son Aaron Wulu's wife Crystal Wulu delivered a baby boy named Aaron Wulu Jr. Being a young couple who were just coming up, our son and his wife sent for us to come to Cleveland to assist them with their young child.

So we honored their request and moved to Cleveland at the earlier part of November 1994. Even my wife, Minnie Wulu, was with them in October before November, in order to help them take care of their child. I told my wife that Aaron took advice, so we must assist him to do whatever he wanted us to do now while we were still strong by the grace of God.

When Aaron Wulu got his first job in Cleveland, I advised him, "The first important thing you should think about is to buy a house, because your papa and mommy owned a home before you were born. It pays to have your own home, because when you do, no one can bother you and you can sleep in peace." Keeping the advice in mind, Aaron bought a two-family building on Parkview Avenue in 1993.

When we moved to Cleveland, we did not border about where to stay. Aaron B. Wulu gave us the second floor apartment of his house. We were very pleased and happy. While helping our son and his wife with their baby, we did attend the Day Care Training in Cleveland, Ohio, because we decided to take care of working mothers' children.

Even though we had previously taken up Day Care Training in Detroit, Michigan, and not in Cleveland, Ohio, we were advised by the Social Service Department that we had to take the training again. So we did what the Social Service Department told us to do. My wife received a Day Care certificate after the completion of the training.

With anxiety to work for ourselves and have our own business, we opened our Day Care Center at the home of Aaron Wulu at 9418 Parkview Avenue, Cleveland, Ohio, during the latter part of 1995. We named the center the Minnie Wulu Day Care Center.

The Miracles and Riches of God

At the Minnie Wulu Day Care Center, we took care of many American children. We were grateful to God, who gave us the strength to render our service in the educational field of child care.

It is good to have your own business. We were able to get a loan and purchased a two-family house on Parkview Avenue through our Minnie Wulu Day Care business. In August 1997, we purchased the home and moved in December of the same year. We were thankful to the Almighty that He blessed us to have our own home in America. We used the first floor for our Day Care services.

The Minnie Wulu Day Care helped our son Aaron and his wife with their four children. It was really God's blessing that we were around them while they were having their children. They went to work while we cared for their children.

Our Day Care is next to Aaron's home. Our Day Care helped Kaller Mckay with her children also.

With ambition and determination to be a citizen of United States, I earnestly prayed to the Lord and started studying Immigration Law and American history. I then attended classes on Euclid Avenue near downtown Cleveland.

I took the examination and passed. I received a certificate which proved that I had passed the citizenship requirement test.

In view of the above mentioned, I put in an application for citizenship. Later, the Bureau of Immigration sent for me for an interview. I attended the interview and passed the test. The Bureau of Immigration and Naturalization wrote me to come to the court on January, 16, 1998, in downtown Cleveland to be sworn in as a citizen of United States of America. With happiness and joy in my heart, I went to downtown Cleveland to the court and was sworn in as a citizen of United States on January 16, 1998.

God is good. He helped me in many ways. It is my duty to tell every person who will read my life's story that the best thing to do under the

117

John Nimley Wulu, Sr., AA,BA

sun is to pray to God day and night, because He gives wisdom and understanding and strength.

Remember, prayer is the key that opens heaven's door. Daniel prayed three times a day and God showed him visions and he was able to interpret dreams. So in this world, it pays to pray day and night. Through prayer and trust in Almighty God, we lived happily in our house for six years and did Day Care comfortably. In 2002, November 28 was Thanksgiving Day. My birthday happens to fall on that same day. We had a grand Thanksgiving Day celebration at the home of Mr. and Mrs. Mckay (my son-in-law and daughter). We thanked and praised God for his protection and his blessings upon us.

My birthday on November 28, 2002, was a very good one. Dr. John T. Wulu Jr. was the master of the Thanksgiving celebration. He gave thanks and praise to God for protecting and blessing the family. He introduced his sisters and brothers: Elizabeth, Ruth, Emanuel, Francois-Caesar, Solomon, Kaller-Minnie, Demonique-Alexander, Johnnette, and Aaron. Dr. John T. Wulu Jr. introduced himself in fourth place as the Lord brought them in the world. He also introduced their children.

All my children who were present gave me birthday gifts. Dr. John T. Wulu Jr. and his family gave $200, Elizabeth Wulu Brown and her family gave $100, Aaron B. Wulu and his family gave $100 on the spot and pledged $500 for my house mortgage, which he gave later. That made his birthday gift to me $600. My son-in-law Joseph Mckay and my daughter Kaller-Minnie Mckay gave $100 for my birthday. My daughter, Mrs. Kaller-Minnie Mckay, pledged to buy a house for my wife and me. She said she was very pleased that the Lord was protecting us.

My granddaughter Lakisha Bondurant gave $100 cash and prepared food worth $100, and Mrs. Greta Williams, Kaller's friend, gave $5.

My grandson Eddie Wulu read a statement and presented it to me. It read, "To the Greatest Grandfather I ever had in my life. You have

The Miracles and Riches of God

been a great influence for all of us. We appreciate you for bringing us here and giving us more opportunities for our education and a better life. We are all blessed to have such a strong man in our lives. Happy birthday and we wish you many, many more to come. We love you. Eddie Wulu." After receiving the fine birthday gifts from my children, grandchildren, and other well-wishers, I took in their kind remarks. I then expressed my thanks and appreciation in the following manner.

Mommy and Papa Wulu had dinner for Elizabeth and her mission team from the United States in May 2007. Mission team included Dana Carpenter, Chris and Id Lafe'

Papa Wulu, Mommy, Principal Kennedy, and Vice Principal Otis and teacher

School on Bushrod Island near St. Paul Bridge. Mommy & Papa Wulu took picture with Principal, teachers and students

Me and my wife's 50th wedding anniversary group picture
--2004.

Left to right: Solomon, Josephine, Dr. Wulu, Jr., and Mommy Wulu

Left to right: Mommy Wulu, Papa Wulu, school Queen and Chief Registrar, James Tarwayson.

Chapter 11

A WORD OF GRATITUDE FOR GOD'S MANY BLESSINGS

My dear wife, Mrs. Minnie Wulu

My dear children and spouses

Brothers and sisters in Christ

Ladies and Gentlemen:

Today is a great and unique occasion for all of us who are present here on this Thanksgiving Day.

Our main purpose of this gathering is to thank Almighty God and to glorify His name for His love and protection. We are here especially to thank God for giving us His only begotten Son Christ Jesus, through whom we have received the blessings of life.

I believe we all have the knowledge of John 3:16, which says, "For God so loved the world that he gave His only begotten Son, that whosoever believeth on Him shall not perish but have everlasting life." To be frank, I believe on the Lord Jesus Christ and I am saved. My dear children, I urge you to continue your faith in Christ Jesus.

It is very obvious that we all receive our many blessings from God through our Lord Jesus Christ, the Savior of the world. Christ shared his blood for you and me to save us from our sins. If it was not for the Gospel of Christ (the Good News), we would not have the glorious

John Nimley Wulu, Sr., AA, BA

opportunity to be here today. Let us give God the glory for Jesus Christ.

Christian brothers and sisters, I praise God for the gospel of His Son, which enables me to be where I am today. The Gospel of Jesus Christ paved the way for eternal life. Let us give praises to the Father.

Today I am happy to thank God for my dear wife, Minnie Wulu, who stood by my side in all of my ups and downs for the past forty-eight years.

My dear wife, I am very grateful to you. Our Lord God has blessed us with riches (our children). Our children are indeed a blessing from the Lord.

Special thanks to you for all the good you have done for me and the care you continue to give me through the help of God. I praise God for giving you the strength to bring forth our wonderful loving children.

And now to all of my dear children, grand- and great-grandchildren, you are our blessings and riches from God. I thank God for all of you. I thank him for bringing you safely into the world through us. You should always thank the Lord for His continuous guidance and protection over your lives. He is your Creator and Protector. God is the giver of your many blessings.

To my daughters and sons-in-law, I thank the Lord for putting you in our family. You have been a blessing to our children.

Put your trust in God and He will continue to bless you. I appreciate you, and many thanks for standing with our children.

Young people, put God first in all you do in this world. Put your confidence and trust in Him. Remember your mother and father because it is through them you came into this world. Think of your parents because they have given you great care from the day you were born until maturity. Your parents helped you and prayed for your safety. They gave you good advice of being good, honest, and respectful.

This is a very happy day for me, ladies and gentlemen. I am looking at the faces of my beautiful daughters and daughters-in-law and handsome

The Miracles and Riches of God

sons and son-in-law. I am very happy and pleased to see all of you and your children here today.

To my married children, God has put you and your spouses together. I pray that by the grace of God you go beyond the forty-eight years my wife and I have been married. Thank you very highly for being good partners. Please remember, you are one flesh according to the Word of God.

Now on this Thanksgiving Day, I believe it is my obligation to call upon you and remind you about family unity. Family unity is good and very important. Where there is unity, there is peace. I want our Family unity to grow stronger.

Love your brothers and sisters with pure heart. Protect your sisters and brothers. Children, you all are one blood. Love your mother and father and relatives. It is God's will that you love one another. By this the world will know that you are one.

Good people, please give me your ears and hear. I want to express my special thanks and appreciation to all of our children and grandchildren for the great help they have given to us in the past and the assistance they continue to give us. Children, on behalf of my dear wife and myself, and from the depth of my heart, I thank ALL OF YOU for your great assistance to your mother and me. Thank you for your good deeds toward us while we are still alive.

I pray that the good Lord rewards you for caring for us. I also pray that God pays you back double for all you have given us. I also thank God for all our grandchildren, especially our first grandson, Darlington T. Wulu, who is following in the footsteps of his aunts and uncles in providing our needs.

I give God the honor and praise for all of your good deeds.

It is now my prerogative to draw your kind attention again as I am coming to the end of my speech. Be good citizens. Each one of you must value yourself as a person of good character; have strong ambition and determination.

John Nimley Wulu, Sr., AA,BA

Spend your time on a worthy cause which will result in a beneficial achievement in the interest of people and your country.

Aim high always as you prepare yourselves at all times for a better future. A better tomorrow is for those who prepare themselves through education and training and have meaningful skills. You are young and strong and have a great opportunity to do so.

May I say to you all, my good people, today is the day to praise God. I thank God for all of us. Let us have an enjoyable day.

Thanks and may our God bless us all.

John N. T. Wulu Sr.

The Thanksgiving celebration in 2002 was very good. We ate and enjoyed ourselves, and after my speech we took various group pictures.

Within the period of a few months, Mrs. Kaller Wulu Mckay bought a two-room brick house for us. The deed was in her name. In October of 2003 we moved into the house and were very pleased.

Our Lord God is good. When we moved to Kaller's house, we were caring for two of her children. In November, she gave birth to a baby boy, Benjamin, November 16, 2003. This meant we would have three of her children to care for.

While we were happy about the birth of baby boy Benjamin, our son, Dr. John T. Wulu Jr., and his pretty wife, Josephine Wulu, invited us and hosted our fiftieth wedding anniversary at their beautiful home in Mitchellville, Maryland. We are very grateful to them. Their kind deed we pray not to forget.

No one knows the future, only the merciful God knows our future. After we moved into Kaller's house, our happiness was short lived, because of circumstances beyond our control. We had no choice, and we had to move out. So we left her house at the later part of September 2004.

126

The Miracles and Riches of God

Our God is good. He makes a way for anyone who trusts in Him and looks to Him for assistance. As God would have it, our son Demonique Wilson, who lives in Great Britain, had a son. He sent for us to come and help him and his wife care for their baby boy, Demonique Wilson Jr. Demonique's wife, Thabo delivered on October 10, 2004. They believed that we could teach them how to care for their baby because God had shown us how to care for our ten living children besides our many grandchildren.

We were grateful to the Lord and then we left Cleveland, Ohio, and went to Dr. John T. Wulu Jr. in Mitchellville, Maryland, in order to travel to Salford, Manchester, Great Britain. We stayed three weeks and some days at the home of Dr. Wulu before leaving. Demonique Wilson paid for two round-trip tickets for us to go to him. On October 26, 2004, with happiness in our hearts, we flew to the United Kingdom to our son Demonique Wilson. My wife, Minnie Wulu, and I arrived at Manchester Airport at 7:00 a.m., October 27, 2004.

Our son Demonique Wilson and his wife were pleased to see us. My wife, Minnie Wulu, was pleased to be in Great Britain for two important reasons: to seek dental treatment and to teach our son and his wife how to care for their young baby boy. I was there to seek a medical doctor for my hearing problem. The doctor helped me by repairing my hearing aid. I also enjoyed my birthday on November 28, 2004, at the home of Demonique Wilson, and I received a birthday gift of $400 from my son Demonique and his wife. I thank God for them.

After staying some weeks in Great Britain, I came back to the United States in December 2004. I went back at the middle part of January 2005 and stayed there for some weeks and returned to the United States.

Great Britain is a very beautiful place. My wife and I enjoyed our visit there. We traveled by train from Salford, Manchester, to London. We stayed in London for two days. We traveled by train to go and see Buckingham Palace, the official home of the King and Queen of

127

John Nimley Wulu, Sr., AA,BA

England. We saw many lion statues and many fountains of spring water.

My wife and I returned in March 2005 to the United States with great happiness because we had seen a great country. In the United Kingdom, the people use pounds for currency. During our visit, I noticed that one pound was equal to US$2. Fifty pounds was equivalent to US$100.

When we came back, we landed at Washington Airport, and Dr. John T. Wulu Jr. and his wife picked us up at the airport and took us to their house in Mitchellville, Maryland, and we stayed there three days and left. We came to Cleveland, Ohio, where we have our own home on Parkview Avenue.

We like Cleveland because we have property there, and some of our children live there. Most of our grandchildren live in Cleveland. My wife and I also love Cleveland because that is where we got our green cards and where we became naturalized citizens of the United States.

In addition, three of our ten children got their green cards in Cleveland and also became naturalized and got their citizenship there. Four of our children owned properties in Cleveland. We live in peace and happiness in Cleveland, Ohio.

The United States is a great and good country. There are some good people in Cleveland. Some of the good people who helped us in this country are Pastor William Sander of True Light Worship Center, Pastor Orum T. Trone, and lady Stephanie of Detroit, Michigan. Some of the good people who help us in Cleveland, Ohio, are John W. Brown, Joseph Mckay, Pastor McJunkin and Pastor Ronald E. Maxwell, and the members of Affinity Baptist Church. These are just some of the good American people whose kind deeds touched me.

CHAPTER 12
THE HONOR PROGRAM

The administration of our school, Richard M. Nixon Institute, honored my wife and me on the school campus as they observed their 43rd Gala Anniversary on Thursday, May 24, 2007.

At the honoring celebration, Principal Kennedy expressed that the administration deemed it necessary to honor us for our numerous services rendered in the field of education in Liberia. He stated, "You have shown your interest in education by erecting concrete school buildings and establishing schools in Liberia."

Mr. Kennedy also expressed special thanks to us for providing schools where students have the opportunity to get an education and teachers are privileged to obtain employment, enabling them to impart their skilled knowledge to students, young and old.

It was a grand occasion. With smiles and a happy spirit, the administration, faculty, staff, and student body honored us by gowning my wife, Mrs. Minnie Wulu, and I during the indoor ceremony on parade day.

After being gowned with smiling faces, I expressed special thanks and appreciation to the administration, faculty staff, and student body for honoring us with their kind interest in Richard M. Nixon Institute, John Wulu Elementary and Junior High, and John Wulu Kindergarten

John Nimley Wulu, Sr., AA,BA

School in Monrovia, Liberia. I further told the students that a better tomorrow is for those who prepare themselves for it.

I give praise and glory to God of our Lord Jesus Christ, who gives me wisdom, understanding, and strength to write my story. I thank God for all He has done for me from the very day He put me in my mother's womb. I thank him for all He will do for me in the future. I earnestly pray and ask all my children, grandchildren, and great-grand children and their children until eternity to live their lives for Christ and follow the way of God, who blessed us and whom all mankind look up to for blessings and protection.

John Nimley Wulu, Sr., AA,BA

Printed in the United States
137647LV00004B/55/P